T0082472

Self-Care
for
Latinas

Self-Care for Latinas

100+ Ways to Prioritize & Rejuvenate Your Mind, Body, & Spirit

Raquel Reichard

ADAMS MEDIA

New York   London   Toronto   Sydney   New Delhi

Aadamsmedia

Adams Media
An Imprint of Simon & Schuster, Inc.
100 Technology Center Drive
Stoughton, Massachusetts 02072

First Adams Media hardcover edition
December 2023

ADAMS MEDIA and colophon are
registered trademarks of Simon &
Schuster, Inc.

For information about special
discounts for bulk purchases, please
contact Simon & Schuster Special
Sales at 1-866-506-1949 or
business@simonandschuster.com.

The Simon & Schuster Speakers Bureau
can bring authors to your live event. For
more information or to book an event,
contact the Simon & Schuster Speakers
Bureau at 1-866-248-3049 or visit our
website at www.simonspeakers.com.

Interior design by Priscilla Yuen
Illustrations by Stephanie Vidal

Manufactured in the United States
of America

10 9 8 7 6 5 4 3 2 1

Library of Congress Cataloging-in-
Publication Data has been applied for.

ISBN 978-1-5072-2142-6
ISBN 978-1-5072-2143-3 (ebook)

Many of the designations used by
manufacturers and sellers to distinguish
their products are claimed as trademarks.
Where those designations appear in
this book and Simon & Schuster, Inc.,
was aware of a trademark claim, the
designations have been printed with initial
capital letters.

To my mami and your mami.
To my niece and your daughter.
To you, to me, to us.
To breaking generational cycles
and a culture of marianismo by
choosing to care for ourselves.

Contents

6

part one
Mind / 27

part two
Body / 81

Index / 188

INTRODUCTION

Amorcita, close your eyes, take a few calming breaths, and identify how you feel. What are the thoughts running through your mind? ¿Qué sientes en tu cuerpo? How is your spirit? Now open your eyes, and be real with yourself. If you felt anxious, overwhelmed, or even unsure *what* you felt, you're not alone.

And, hermana, this is precisely why prioritizing self-care is essential. Due to factors like chronic stress and acculturation, Latinas have higher rates of depression, eating disorders, and suicidal ideation than non-Latine white women. Más allá, we have a shorter life expectancy than most women: Latinas die at higher rates from cervical cancer and may be at greater risk for cardiovascular and cerebrovascular diseases. Taking care of your mind, body, and spirit will help you overcome these obstacles and reclaim the power that is innately yours.

After all, you (or your ancestors) come from a land where women just like you were divine healers who understood the mind-body-soul connection. But along the way, you, y probablemente tu mamá y tu abuela, forgot. It's not your fault. Hundreds of years ago, that magic in your lineage was stolen by colonizers who viewed your knowledge as a threat. Today your ancient wisdom and practices are whitewashed, packaged, and sold at wildly high prices to a target market that doesn't include you. Life is hard. Y mija, para ti, a woman juggling the demands of work, home, and life in a society hell-bent on making everything harder because of your ethnicity, race, immigration status, language, class, and/or gender, 'chacha, la cosa está brutal. But you don't have to let these challenges defeat you. You can choose another path.

Self-Care for Latinas is here to help. You'll find more than a hundred self-care activities designed by and for Latinas to cultivate your sense of mental, physical, and spiritual wellness, such as:

- *Unlearn the lies marianismo taught you.*
- *Turn reggaetón lyrics into affirmations.*
- *Rebuild your relationship with cultural foods.*
- *Embark on your señora era.*
- *Set boundaries and honor them.*

Some exercises will resonate more with you than others. After all, despite a shared cultural background, Latinas don't lead identical lives. Some make more money. Some are parents. Some have intersecting marginalized identities, like race, immigration status, gender presentation, and sexuality, that compound and make it even more challenging to carve out time for self-care.

But here's the thing: You're all worthy of self-care and deserve to take time to nourish yourself—mind, body, and soul. Restore your health and well-being one simple activity at a time with *Self-Care for Latinas*. Dale, let s get started.

LETTER TO THE READER

Dear Reader,

Hi, sweet loves! If you picked up this book, you're likely interested in learning self-care practices that feel culturally relevant to you as someone with roots in Latin America or the Caribbean. As you know, this beautiful region of wondrous terrain, vibrant spirits, complicated politics, and violent colonial histories is made up of people of various races, languages, and cultures.

I, a light-skinned Puerto Rican cis woman who grew up in a Spanglish, lower-income home in the southern US city of East Orlando, Florida, write from my context, one that is likely distinct from yours. Throughout the pages of this book, I sprinkle in Caribbean Spanish, Nuyorican Spanglish, and southern slang, vernacular that is natural to me considering my family's migrational journeys. I'm cognizant that my language and experiences are not universal, and yet, despite our differences, I believe that the lessons and practices offered in this book could help you on your path toward healing and self-care.

I also want to keep it real with you. While I was writing *Self-Care for Latinas*, there were many times when impostor syndrome crept in, demanding to know, Who am I to write about self-care? But I reminded myself how that voice withheld key information, like how I've dedicated my decade-long career as a journalist to covering Latina body politics and wellness. That's the thing about the chatter in our heads: It intentionally leaves out critical details so that we can believe its self-sabotaging lies. It was through some of the techniques I discuss in this book that I was able to work through my own self-doubt and write what I hope will be a tool kit you can use to help build your own sense of mental, physical, and spiritual wellness.

While you're on this journey, I need you to know that we, amores, are living, breathing women with a myriad of emotions that come, go, return for longer, and temporarily disappear until they arise within us once again. This is what it means to be human, mama. And self-care is what allows us to survive life's seesaw so that we can create big, beautiful lives despite it all. So use what works for you now and hold on to what doesn't, because ¿quién sabe?, it may be helpful during life's next sway.

Raquel

WHY LATINAS MUST PRACTICE SELF-CARE

Latinas are bad, ain't we? I don't mean this in the spicy, femme fatale way we've been stereotyped as for generations, though yeah, we are damn fine too. What I mean is that we are extraordinary in numerous ways. Many of us trace our histories to Indigenous women warriors who battled ruthless colonizers; African women who maintained their spiritualities, tongues, and ways of life at a time when these practices were outlawed; or the few mestizo women who used their racial, economic, and educational privileges to advance women's rights for those across their Latin American and Caribbean countries and territories. In our bodies and our spirits, we are our ancestors' divine legacy—the living, breathing, and multiplying prize of struggles waged and won.

But many of us are still fighting. Every day, we wake up in a world that systemically and institutionally harms us. According to Tanya Katerí Hernández's 2022 book *Racial Innocence: Unmasking Latino Anti-Black Bias and the Struggle for Equality*, Black Latinas are more likely to be denied access to work and housing. Undocumented Latinas are often exploited and abused by their employers. The Williams Institute at the UCLA School of Law reports that transgender Latinas have a greater risk of being stopped and criminalized by law enforcement; and when incarcerated, they often experience violence when housed with men. On the street, our bodies are hypersexualized. We are viewed as perpetually available for public consumption, putting us at greater risk of sexual violence. At least one-third of Latinas experience intimate partner violence. On the news and in TV shows and movies, our communities are shown as threats to social order: brown foreigners birthing so-called "anchor babies" in the Southwest, menacing Black street kids in northeastern inner cities, and loose girls with bad morals and even lousier tongues in the Southeast.

The media dehumanizes us, compelling us to internalize the myths of our inferiority. We grow to despise the color of our skin, the depth of our cheekbones, the texture of our hair, the shape of our bodies. We become embarrassed by the sound of our mother's accent, or the nameplate necklace she spent her savings on to gift to us back when we were carefree nenitas, unashamed of the sacred beauty we'd blasphemously be taught to hate.

And amid these external and internal battles, Latinas are expected to carry on. As we say in my matria Puerto Rico, la brega continúa. So we continue to put in long hours at work and accomplish great things despite discrimination and impostor syndrome. We provide physical and emotional care to our families and friends, mentor young people, and participate in local protests and town halls to create change within our communities. With every minute of our days accounted for, our agendas feel too crammed to book time for ourselves. So we continue bregando in the name of survival, silently killing ourselves instead.

Too heavy? I hear you. But know what's even heavier? The loads of responsibility, untreated trauma, and self-hate you're carrying on your shoulders. It's weighing you down, love—physically, mentally, and spiritually—and it's hurting you in material and nonmaterial ways.

Let's start with those work and life duties. When your day is so jam-packed that you're holding in your pee for as long as you can and avoiding getting up to refill your water bottle because you just don't have the minute to spare, you're likely to experience burnout. When you're swamped, you feel overwhelmed, drained, and unable to complete even the most basic task. Burnout causes mental, physical, and emotional stress. Physically, it has been linked to heart disease, diabetes, gastrointestinal issues, high cholesterol, and colds and flus. Mentally, it can lead to insomnia, anxiety, and depressive symptoms.

In addition to burnout, many Latinas are navigating life with untreated traumas. For some, it's stigma that stops us from getting the help we need. For others, it's systemic barriers like finances, health insurance, or the scarcity of therapists who speak our languages. But for many of us, it's simply not being able to identify how our unhealed wounds continue to impact us. When we experience something traumatic, it alters the neural pathways in our brain. These altered pathways influence how we experience the world and cause us to view everyday experiences through a lens of trauma and fear. As a result, some of us experience insomnia or have nightmares and frequent panic attacks. Others develop mental health conditions like eating disorders (ED), obsessive-compulsive disorder (OCD), post-traumatic stress disorder (PTSD), and dissociative disorders, among other mental illnesses. Physically, untreated traumas can lead to low energy, headaches, chronic pain, cardiovascular disease, and gastrointestinal distress.

Finally, there's self-hate, or what psychologists sometimes call self-loathing. It describes our extreme self-criticism; those feelings that we are not good enough, smart enough, or pretty enough; that belief that our lives carry less value and, thus, we are unworthy of the good things that other people and communities receive. These ideas don't come out of thin air. They are learned. For some, these lessons were taught by families who neglected and abused us. For others, they were communicated to us by a society that treats us unfairly and a popular culture that portrays us as a grotesque second class of scheming villains.

Regardless of where you learned to hate yourself, the impact remains dangerous. It robs you of living a full life and cheats you from thriving in your purpose. Self-loathing can also lead to depression, social anxiety, body image issues, and eating disorders. It can even cause self-isolation, where you, alone in your room or apartment, stop moving your body, making you more vulnerable to physical illnesses.

Like I said, sis: The weight of your weekly planner, untreated traumas, and self-hate is heavy, and it's crushing you. But there is a panacea: self-care. Self-care is about nurturing and nourishing yourself. It means taking the time (or making the time) to do things that revitalize you so that you can live well. It can look like removing some of the weight from your shoulders so that it's easier for you to carry. Or maybe it's temporarily putting the load down so that you can rest, replenish, and lift it again, sustainably. Hopefully, it's a bit of both. After all, self-care isn't just one thing. It's about caring for all of you: your mind, your body, and your spirit. In fact, a growing body of research is showing that there is a mind-body-soul connection, and when one (or more) of these is out of alignment, it affects the others.

The Reasons Self-Care Is So Important

Everyone needs to practice self-care, especially you, mami. Research has found that women of color experience health stressors that are directly tied to race, gender, and ancestral trauma.

According to Columbia University professor Robert T. Carter, when we—especially Black and Indigenous Latinas—confront microaggressions, prejudice, discrimination, and violence because of our race (or how our ethnicity has been racialized), we can experience a type of PTSD. This can look like us avoiding people, places, and activities out of fear of violence or discrimination, or being hyper-aware of how we present and move in spaces that have historically been unkind, or even dangerous, to us or people like us. It makes it difficult to just be present in our bodies because we feel like we are under surveillance and threat, regardless of whether or not we actually are.

Under a patriarchal society where men have historically held power, women have had to face various disparities. Women suffer sexism in the form of a gender pay gap, diminishing reproductive healthcare, gender violence, and unattainable beauty ideals. The sexism we as Latinas encounter is often compounded by issues related to race, ethnicity, and/or culture. The wage gap is wider for us than it is for non-Latine white women, and our communities are usually among the hardest hit when our reproductive rights are rescinded. Even more, we confront gender roles and expectations from both of our cultures, including the machismo and marianismo of our countries of origin, as well as the racialized and/or xenophobic sexism we encounter in the lands we've migrated to around the world. All of this impacts our well-being. It makes it harder to navigate the world in our bodies, causing us unnecessary stress. Additionally, it contributes to our internalization of racism, sexism, and xenophobia that too often leads to our self-hate.

As if that weren't enough, emerging research is finding that the traumatic events that our ancestors endured could impact us as well, even if we did not personally experience them. Ancestral trauma posits that if your parents or ancestors lived through traumatic events, then you, too, could feel the repercussions. This concept was first explored by psychiatrist Dr. Vivian M. Rakoff in 1966, who found that the offspring of Holocaust survivors experienced negative mental health outcomes, not unlike those who had suffered under the Nazis. More recently, clinical psychologist Dr. Joy DeGruy has studied how the enslavement of Africans in the United States continues to impact the habits, practices, behaviors, perspectives, and fears of Black Americans today.

Ancestral trauma has been attributed to both internal and external factors. Scientists who study epigenetics, an area that probes how people's environments and behaviors can affect how their genes work, have found that ancestral trauma can alter the DNA structure in the progeny of trauma victims in a process called epigenetic inheritance. As many Black Latinas are the descendants of enslaved Africans, 90 percent of whom were taken to Latin America and the Caribbean, and Indigenous Latinas come from communities that survived genocide, it's also likely that these Latinas could experience a form of ancestral trauma. The same could be said of those whose ancestors lived through other traumatic experiences.

How and When to Practice Self-Care

It's time to start healing. To do this, you need to prioritize your well-being. You need to take care of yourself. You need to practice self-care, and you need to ensure that you focus on your mind, body, and soul. And guess what: You need to start now. You can't keep putting off your well-being for some day in the future when your schedule clears. It won't be clear until you adopt the tools and exercises to help you create more balance in your life. This work takes time, so start today and commit to practicing at least one self-care exercise or action every day. Yeah, ma, todos los días. I'll show you how. The self-care ideas in this book are broken down into three categories—mind, body, and spirit—to help you focus your attention on key areas.

MENTAL SELF-CARE

Self-care is multifaceted, but we are starting with the mind because what happens in your head often has a direct impact on your body and soul. The stories you tell yourself have the power to motivate you into physical action or can keep you idle, unable to get out of bed, lolling around in a dingy white T-shirt that belonged to an ex. Bring back any memories?

Speaking of memories, the reason you have to prioritize your mental health is that so much of what you experience throughout your life, and especially during the infancy-to-late-twenties period when your brain is developing, is stored like a shadow in your brain. Your brain carries lessons and memories as well as the emotions tied to them. So, when a person experiences a traumatic event—like watching their father assault their mother, being ripped away from a caretaker by immigration enforcement, or experiencing sexual abuse—the memory is imprinted on the amygdala, the part of the brain that holds the emotional significance of the event. After the trauma, the brain can easily be triggered by sounds, smells, and sights that recall the fear or pain of the experience, whether there is any real physical danger or not. For others, the memories could be hidden in the brain in its attempt to protect against re-experiencing the stress and emotional suffering of recalling the event. But these suppressed memories can still show up through debilitating mental conditions like anxiety, eating disorders, OCD, depression, PTSD, and dissociative disorders.

While traumatic experiences can alter the way you view and move through life, your brain has the power to change and adapt through a process called neuroplasticity. It's like a human superpower, allowing you to rewire your brain and reframe your world. Through healthy mental exercises, like the self-care actions you'll learn and practice in the pages ahead, you can work through the suffering that has been holding you hostage, develop healthful coping strategies, and, ultimately, rewrite your narrative. This, amor, is how you free yourself and create peace, love, and balance in your own mind.

PHYSICAL SELF-CARE

Your brain isn't the only part of your body that stores those painfully debilitating experiences of your past; your body does too. Your body cells hold an imprint of your past traumatic events and, when left unprocessed, this can make you susceptible to physical ailments.

Think about how your body usually responds when you are mentally unwell. Maybe your stomach hurts when you're anxious. Or you get a headache when you're enraged. Or you have trouble sleeping when you're grieving. Your body reacts physically to how you feel emotionally, and paying attention to the sensations that arise allows you to decode the messages your body is sharing with you about what it needs to be healthy. It could be asking you to eat, rest, cry, or move. If you don't listen, or ignore your body's intelligence and calls for care, you become susceptible to severe physical health conditions, like strokes, heart attacks, diabetes, and cancer.

Culturally, we've been taught to minimize the aches and pains in our bodies. We've seen our mamis work through physical agony because they felt like they couldn't risk missing work. We've watched our tías drink soups and teas like medicine to soothe the symptoms of untreated illnesses. It's time to end this cycle of shrugging off or only praying away pain, and instead shower your body with the love and care it deserves by listening to it and giving it the rest and/or movement it's asking for.

SPIRITUAL SELF-CARE

When you care for yourself mentally and physically, your spiritual health is able to thrive. In fact, many world religions refer to bodies as holy temples that must be honored, understanding that spiritual well-being is tied to the health of the vessel containing it. But spiritual work isn't exclusive to the pious. Whether you follow a religion or spiritual practice or not, your inner being—your soul's voice, as author and therapist Christine Gutierrez calls it—needs to be heard so that your spirit can be properly cared for.

Your soul is the part of you that has always existed. It's the part of you that felt sad when someone swatted an insect even after it bit you. It's the part of you that stood up for the kid being bullied at school (or felt guilty for not having the courage to say something). It's the part of you that dreams about sprawling among a field of girasoles or bathing in a waterfall that runs through your home country. Your soul is the part of you that is connected to the universe and to the energy in all life—land, animal, and human.

Taking care of your spirit allows you to stay connected to that which you can't see. Trauma, grief, hate, and violence rupture these relationships. You become confused, believing you are alone in your despair. Soul work reminds you that you are not alone—that your fulfillment, your purpose, and your equilibrium emerge when you are in community with the spirits that surround you.

Taking care of your soul can sound like a silent prayer or like yelling the lyrics to a song by La India in your car. It's making sure you are feeding your spirit with una cucharita de abuelita's sopita daily. Taking care of your soul is how you fall in love with yourself and your life. It's what gives you the permission to be your full self and respect your mind and body as they are, ever changing, ever growing, and ever dazzling.

You Deserve Tender, Revolutionary Self-Care

Self-care is transformative. Self-care has the power to heal and revive—and you are so deserving of resurrection, mi amor. You owe it to yourself to go all in so that you can experience lasting change. This doesn't mean that the roads stop winding or that you go through life without the baggage of your past. It means you can better navigate the turns ahead and can transfer the load on your back to one of those maletas with the spinner wheels. You know, the fancy ones.

Scholar Gloria Anzaldúa once said, "I change myself, I change the world." And in so many ways, this is what self-care is all about. Self-care is making the decision to choose yourself in a world and culture that tell you as a Latina that you should be self-sacrificial. But who does your self-immolation serve? Not you, not your community, and not the generations that will follow you. Writer and professor Audre Lorde defined self-care as "an act of political warfare." It's "self-preservation" so that you can continue breathing, moving, creating, loving, laughing, and showing up for yourself and each other in a menacing world.

Self-care is intrinsically tied to community care. If you choose to heal, you interact with all living beings more kindly. When you break unhealthy family cycles, you mark the end of ancestral traumas. And when you speak to yourself affectionately, you gift the next generation of Latinas with a sense of self-love and self-worth. It's time, mi vida. It's time to prioritize your well-being, and I'm honored to be the one who treks with you down a path of tender, revolutionary self-care.

part one
Mind

Everyone experiences moments of anguish and despair, and Latinas are no exception. This section is designed to support you in working through mental stressors and emotional wounds. On the following pages, you'll find suggested actions, exercises, and coping strategies to help you deal with, navigate, and process psychological and emotional strains.

As a Latina, some of these practices may be new to you. Even the tips you might've heard before may not have been modeled to you. Allow this section to be your guide. Some actions will encourage you to treat yourself with rest or play, because respite is absolutely critical to your mental well-being. Others will require you to dig deep and confront traumas you have (understandably) been avoiding for a long time. This process won't always feel comfortable, but with patience and practice it will lead you to healing and growth.

As you know, the challenges, microaggressions, triggers, and cultural expectations that arise in the daily lives of Latinas never seem to stop. To counter these, you'll find tips that are made to fit into your everyday schedule. This tool kit of healthful exercises and strategies will help you work through trauma, minimize stressful situations, and find mental calm whenever and wherever you need to. It's time to prioritize your mental health. Ya es tiempo.

Destigmatize Mental Health

It's a part of many mental wellness campaigns these days: Mental health conditions don't discriminate. But growing up in a Latine home, you're taught a different lesson: Esas son cosas de gringos—white American people's problems. When someone within your community happens to prove this mistaken cultural theory wrong by displaying any form of mental distress, it's at best minimized to "los nervios"—the jitters, their nerves acting up—and at worst gets them labeled "una loca."

In both cases, it's rare the individual gets the support they actually need. While Latines show similar susceptibility to mental illness as other communities, we are less likely to receive care. According to the National Alliance on Mental Illness, about 35 percent of Latine adults with mental illness get treatment, compared to the US average of 46 percent. This means that more than half of the Latines who are struggling with conditions like anxiety, depression, PTSD, eating disorders, suicidal ideation, and other mental illnesses are *not* receiving treatment; and without adequate help, these conditions often worsen.

Don't get me wrong. The reasons for this disproportion in care don't entirely fall on Latines. We face several barriers to mental health treatment beyond social stigma—financial, cultural, and linguistic, to name a few. But in order to destigmatize mental health, you first have to understand that anyone—regardless of race, ethnicity, language, immigration status, class, or sexual orientation—can experience mental illness. And that includes me and you, amor. Acknowledgment is the first step toward healing. Normalize talking about mental health and use compassionate language when doing so. Finally, detach seeking professional help from weakness and shame, and recognize it for the powerful act of self-love that it is.

Release the Guilt That Comes with Self-Care

For Latinas, the act of caring for yourself usually comes with a sickening side of guilt. And that mindset is understandable when you think about how many Latinas were raised by elders who toiled day and night, weekday and weekend. You may have watched as people who looked like you, who informed your habits and core beliefs, labored without rest. So you internalized the idea that this is what you must do as well, this is what survival looks like, this is what life as a Latina is. It doesn't help that some parts of the wellness industry have distorted self-care into a marketing scheme for high-priced skin moisturizers, Instagrammable cottage retreats, and $20 smoothies.

Even if you can afford to stop, breathe, and rest, you may believe that you have no right to. When you grow up watching your family sacrifice their health, hours, and joy to create opportunities for you, you might feel like self-care is undeserved and shameful. But it's not.

In taking the time to nourish yourself—mind, body, and spirit— you aren't just honoring your needs and desires—you're honoring theirs as well. When you come up for air, you show them that their sacrifices weren't in vain. When you rest, you empower them to do the same while giving them the tools to do so. And when you allow yourself to recharge, you commit to your self-preservation so that you, like them, can take care of your communities—sustainably.

So stop pushing your body into chronic pain in order to be more productive, and cease apologizing for giving yourself the rest, sustenance, and attention you need and deserve.

Shed Your Scarcity Mindset

A scarcity mindset refers to the fear that you don't have, and will probably never have, enough. For Latinas, this often shows up around work and money: You'll never have enough money to feel like you and your families are financially independent and secure, so you must work multiple jobs, have side gigs, and monetize all of your hobbies and talents. You work yourself to the point of exhaustion—sometimes not because you need to but rather because you fear that at any moment, everything you've worked so hard for will be taken away from you.

This fear is often called irrational, but it's not. In some ways, this panic is generational. Many Latinas grow up in lower-income homes, watching caretakers stress over bills, eating the same plate of white rice and eggs ("comida de pobre," as my papi would say), and being evicted from mobile homes and apartments. When you experience things like this, they're forever imprinted on you. You remember the looks on your loved ones' faces when they broke the news of how your poverty robbed stability from you once again. You remember the fear, uncertainty, embarrassment, and anger you felt. When this is your past, it's natural to have a scarcity mindset. It doesn't matter if you are more financially secure. You know, especially amid what *Forbes* calls a global job security crisis, that this *could* all be taken from you.

But just because something *can* happen doesn't mean that it *will* happen. It's smart to save money and consider multiple streams of income, but it's dangerous when a scarcity mindset dictates your life. Not only does it force you to overwork, pushing your body more than you should, but it also creates unnecessary anxiety that can lead to other mental health conditions, like panic attacks and OCD, as well as physical conditions, like high blood pressure, heart disease, and stomach or gastrointestinal issues.

To start shedding a scarcity mindset, it's important to notice when these fears around lack arise so that you can redirect those thoughts to what you do have. Consider writing in a gratitude journal so that you have a list of prized people, experiences, and items to look back on when you need to be reminded. You don't need a fancy Moleskine notebook, either. An old-school ninety-nine-cent composition book will work just the same. Just be sure to externalize your list from your mind to a paper or digital journal. Physically writing down or typing out what you're grateful for will encourage you to slow down, focus, and reflect more intentionally. Change, of course, doesn't come overnight, but when you do this practice enough times, you begin to interrupt automatic thought patterns and behaviors and create space for positivity and peace.

Breathe In and Exhale

Latinas are stressed tf out. A study by the American Psychological Association found that Latinas are among the most stressed demographic in the country. Day in and day out, you confront stressors small and big. There are the bosses who refer to you as a peppery condiment when you defend yourself, the colleagues who congratulate you for speaking English so well (or for having such a fun accent), and the dates who need to know where you're *really* from. These everyday stings—known as microaggressions—aim to "other" and devalue you. Then there are the things that keep you up at night, tossing and turning, scream-crying into your pillow, like the violence of being separated from loved ones due to an inhumane immigration system, or watching news clips of a natural disaster devastating your homeland and not hearing from your relatives for months.

While you might not be able to implement immigration reform or quit your job tomorrow, you can develop coping mechanisms that can stop you from imploding because of all the stressors. Deep breathing is one of the best ways to quickly lower your stress. Try visualizing yourself lying on a beach, right where the water meets the sand. As you inhale, imagine the wave pulling up onto the shore, gently surrounding your body. As you exhale, release the water back into the ocean. When you breathe deeply, you send a message to your brain to calm down. The brain then takes that little bit of bochinche and spreads it to your body. After a few deep breaths, your heart rate and blood pressure come back down, allowing you to relax in the present moment.

Resist Perfectionism

Remember that scene in *Selena*, the 1997 film about the late Tejano singer, where her father tells her that as Mexican Americans they have to work twice as hard? They have to prove their Mexicanness to those back in their country of origin *and* prove their Americanness in the only country they've ever really known. I'm Puerto Rican, but I've always related to this dialogue—and many Latinas do too.

When the multiple worlds you navigate view you as not enough, you spend your entire life attempting to prove your value through the pursuit of perfectionism. You have to be the perfect daughter, the perfect immigrant, the perfect student, the perfect employee, the perfect boss, the perfect spouse, and the perfect version of yourself because you don't get the same grace for being humanly imperfect as many other folks.

But in this pursuit of perfection, you lose more than you gain. Not only do you place your value in what you can offer others—how much you can produce or how good other people think you are—but you miss out on discovering the parts of yourself that you can only meet by messing up and getting things wrong. When you do something you haven't mastered, something new and challenging, something you could fail at and be critiqued on, you learn and grow. You finally begin to understand that your value doesn't come from what you can do but rather, and simply, from your mere existence.

To resist perfectionism, allow yourself to try new things, especially when they scare you. Stop judging yourself for your mistakes and, instead, embrace your errors, allowing them to teach you—teach you that you can try something new, teach you that you can ask for help, and teach you that the world will keep spinning even when you're not perfect.

Unlearn the Lies
Marianismo Taught You

Harmful messages don't come exclusively from chauvinist filmmakers, bigoted politicians, and the racist neighbors who voted them into office. Oftentimes, the well-meaning people who raised you, even the ones who love you, have influenced the way you think, for better or worse.

Whether consciously or subconsciously, you as a Latina have learned a few limiting beliefs, thoughts, or mindsets from your parents and extended family that you've been taught to believe as absolute truths. Some of the most common ideas might have been rooted in marianismo, a counterpart to the toxic masculinity of machismo, which venerates sexist, gendered virtues. For women, this means interpersonal harmony, inner strength, sexual purity, and self-sacrifice take precedence over self-care and personal fulfillment. Marianismo teaches girls and women that self-immolation is admirable and celebrates the women in your family who sacrifice their dreams and well-being for their partners and families. This, you are taught, is what it means to be a good Latina girl, and there are many Latina women who stay in unhealthy relationships, believe they need to abandon themselves now that they're mothers, and make decisions that are expected of them (even if it's not what they want) because of these attitudes. It's a generational cycle of girlhood that must meet its end, and you're gonna be the one to finish it in your own family.

Here's why: Multiple studies have shown that sexism, like that upheld through marianismo, increases the risk of mental health conditions like depression, psychological distress, and life dissatisfaction.

Limiting beliefs create unnecessary constraints on how you live your life, which could lead to a lack of self-trust, impostor syndrome, and anxiety. All because you're being forced to follow a script of girlhood and womanhood that you didn't even write.

Unlearning the lies marianismo taught you is one of the most freeing things you can do. It allows you to throw out the screenplay and be the lead writer in your own writers' room. To start, identify the ways marianismo has been modeled to you throughout your life. Next, think of how it was expected of you, including the ways you've adhered to it and the times when you, perhaps unbeknownst to yourself, rebelled. What was the outcome? Who got upset? These details are important, because it's likely that these are the people you'll have to set boundaries with as you lead your life free from the role that marianismo cast you in. There may be bumps on the road— folks might push back when you begin to use your voice and make your own rules. Still, always remember you have the right to choose your roles—and how you play them—in your life.

Make Decisions for Yourself— Not Anyone Else

There's this myth that all Latine families are close-knit and move as a unit. It's nice, in theory, but in reality this stereotype is problematic. For starters, it doesn't speak to everyone's experiences, especially the Latinas who grew up neglected and abused by their families. But even in the cases where this dynamic rings true, it often precipitates self-sacrifice and resentment among Latina daughters.

Self-sacrifice is almost always demanded of Latinas, whether it's under the rules of marianismo or as a directive for the eldest daughter. Long before it became a trend on TikTok, the firstborn girls of immigrants have been talking about the eldest daughter syndrome: the unpaid and often unrecognized labor put on las hijas mayores. Tied to marianismo, eldest daughters of immigrants are expected to sacrifice their childhood in order to act as an additional parent to siblings, a mediator in family quarrels, or a financial provider. But even if you aren't the eldest daughter, you've likely made a decision based on familial expectations.

There are so many stories of Latinas abandoning their passions and talents to enter careers their families wanted for them. Or staying in their hometown because they feel guilty being away from relatives who rely on them for emotional and/or financial support (things that shouldn't fall entirely on one person and can still be met at a distance). Or going to church every Sunday with their mom even if they don't exactly share her faith anymore.

Don't get me wrong: It's beautiful to be part of a connected family, blood or chosen, that supports and provides for each other. Community care is intrinsic to your well-being—but only if it's reciprocated. If not, then you're just being taken advantage of, love. Part of supporting someone is encouraging them to be their whole self, following their dreams and making decisions that help them feel like they are living a purpose-driven life, not one dictated by anyone else—even someone who loves them.

Making decisions for yourself after years of following what others have told you to do isn't easy. It's uncomfortable, comes with guilt, and can even bring unwanted conflict. But recognize that this way of living, and the feelings that come with it, are not serving you. Start small. Buy the outfit fulano said doesn't suit you, enjoy the hobby your tío said was impractical, and don't RSVP to the party if you already have plans. Over time, these small acts of independence can help free you from the weight of others' judgment, and clear a path for discovery and growth.

Work Through Religious Trauma

Have you witnessed a woman tolerate infidelity in her marriage out of fear of being ostracized in her church, or worse, the terror of spending an eternity in a pit of fire for divorcing the cheater? Maybe you yourself have felt shame around your sexual body, your sexual orientation, or your gender identity because of your religious experiences. These are examples of religious trauma—symptoms someone experiences as a result of difficult or stressful religious encounters. Religious trauma can look like someone shaming, gaslighting, or dismissing you for having beliefs that differ from church teachings; someone using religious texts to exert power and control over you; or someone minimizing mental health conditions as "sinful" or "weak."

People of all religious and spiritual backgrounds can experience religious trauma. The effects can be severe, leading to extreme self-hatred, shame, and sexual dysfunction. Religious trauma can also make you hypervigilant, instill a sense of perfectionism, or create a feeling of loneliness. In fact, religious trauma can develop into mental health conditions like PTSD, depression, anxiety, OCD, and eating disorders. And, amor, no religious doctrine that claims to save or free you should be causing you so much anguish and suffering.

To be clear: You don't have to abandon your religion entirely if you don't want to. The key is to be aware of how your religion impacts your mental health. But the reality is that there are a lot of people, and especially young women, being told their role in society should be one of submission and self-denial, and who end up spending lifetimes hating themselves for having their very human (and spiritual) needs unmet.

To work through religious trauma, you must first confront the reality that you experienced (or are experiencing) harm. A study published in the journal *Socio-Historical Examination of Religion and Ministry* found that one-third of adults in the US have experienced some sort of religious trauma. So if you are in this group, you are not alone. Next, create healthy boundaries in your relationships. This could look like excusing yourself when the conversation turns religious or finding a church that feels more respectful of your humanity. Remember that exploring what you believe is not turning away from faith, and be kind to yourself if what you discover looks different from what you've been taught. Finally, know that help is available. There are therapists and online communities focused on religious trauma that can help you work through your pain.

Talk to Yourself Like a
Homeboy from the Homeland

Whether you grew up in Latin America or the Caribbean, spent summers there, or have only experienced the matria through oral stories, there's one thing you probably know with full certainty: No one, and I mean *nadie*, can gas you like a homeboy from the homeland.

They start sentences with signifiers like "mi cielo," "mi corazón," "mi amor," "mi vida," and "mi princesa." They give you nicknames like "chula" and "bebesota." They send you bendiciones and also offer some to your parents for making you. They make you feel like you're divine royalty and they are blessed to be in your holy presence—at first, anyway.

While many times this Latine sweet talk is just game, it sure can make a gal feel good about herself. So the next time you need a quick pick-me-up, tap into your memories of the homeboy from the homeland and romance yourself. It may even boost self-confidence, self-sufficiency, and self-love. You can do this by writing yourself a letter, sending yourself a text message, or just looking at yourself in the mirror and speaking as if you are ol' dude from the block. Give yourself all the sweet nothings he promised. Because regardless of their intentions, the words are true, mami. Y tú, dulzura, amor de mis amores, te lo mereces.

Turn Reggaetón Lyrics Into Affirmations— and Repeat Them to Yourself

Practicing affirmations is one of the easiest—and cheapest (it's free!)—ways to boost your mental well-being. Affirmations are short phrases you can repeat to yourself to help you change how you think or feel. While these expressions should feel personal to you, they don't have to come from you. To encourage your self-confidence, you can borrow from writers who have built careers crafting one-liners: reggaetoneres.

Whether rappers like Bad Bunny, Ivy Queen, or Tego Calderón are spitting rhymes that big-up their own prowess, assert their power and beauty, or uplift their communities, they just have a way of making you feel good about being, well, you. To access that mighty and liberating feeling you get when perreando to the latest chart-topper at the club or in your bedroom, turn your favorite lines into affirmations you can repeat to yourself on the daily. Put your favorite reggaetón playlist on shuffle, listen to the words, and jot down the lines that resonate with you on a piece of paper or in your phone. Repeat the lyrics to yourself when you need a confidence boost.

If it helps, feel free to make the affirmation visible in your home. In my bathroom, positioned between my tub and the mirror hanging above my sink, there is a framed word print from Benito's "Me porto bonito." Every time I hop out of the shower and witness the curves I inherited from mami reflecting back at me, the words remind me that I'm a bebesota. It's an affirmation that makes me feel good and prompts me to dance desnuda por toda la casa!

Stop Comparing Yourself to Others

If you grew up in a big Latine family with sisters and girl cousins, chances are you've compared yourself to others. Likely, you were taught to do this because the elders in your family—your parents, tías, or abuelita—did it first. You remember (how could you forget?): One prima was labeled the pretty one, the other was called the smart one, y la otra era la malcriada. Whichever designation you received, regardless if it was a presumptively good or bad one, placed you in a box, telling you who you are and all you can be. It limited you, and probably made you feel like you were lacking in many ways. It may have even incited sibling and/or cousin rivalries, some that might have unintentionally carried into adulthood.

This is what comparison leads to: contention and unhappiness. When you compare yourself to others, you evaluate yourself against others, allowing your own value to go up or, more likely, down depending on how you feel you measure up. Even more, by focusing on not being good enough, smart enough, pretty enough, or fun enough, you become angry with yourself and those who you perceive to be living in abundance, even if this opulence is an illusion constructed by curated and highly filtered images on Instagram.

There are steps you can take to stop comparing yourself to others, regardless of how long you've been doing it. First, identify the areas where you have historically seen yourself as lacking. Next, think of the places or activities that magnify these negative feelings, whether it's when dancing at the club or scrolling on social media. These are your triggers. Ideally you'll want to avoid them completely, but in real life, that's not always possible. Fortunately there are tools you can learn to help you navigate them better. For example, you can:

- *Take a few calming breaths.*
- *Change your surroundings.*
- *Set screen time limits for social media.*
- *Unfollow accounts that make you feel bad about yourself.*
- *Redirect your thoughts to your strengths.*
- *Reflect on all the things in life you are grateful for.*

It's not easy to undo a lifetime of comparison programming, and change won't come overnight, so it's also okay to distract yourself when the feelings of inadequacy are all-consuming. Spend time in nature, get your nails done, or watch a funny show, anything that takes your attention away from your perceived scarcity and allows you to enjoy the infinite gifts in the ordinary.

Heal Your Inner Child

As a Latina, you might have been forced to grow up fast. Your child-like wonder, buoyancy, and joy may have been interrupted by the realities of racism, xenophobia, and/or sexism; the violence of displacement and family separation; or the limits popular culture put on you because of the color of your skin, your immigration status, or the pronunciation of your name. It broke your heart then, and you may still be hurting.

Unknowingly, you carry so much of what happens to you as a child into your adult life. This presence is sometimes called your inner child. If you experienced pain, trauma, and neglect as a kid, your inner child may feel perpetually vulnerable, scared, and small. It's because of this that self-care must include healing the baby girl that still aches within you. It means facing traumas that haunt you, even some that you've been spending a lifetime running away from. It's difficult, messy, and terrifying, but it's absolutely necessary. You, and that little girl inside of you, deserve a future where you are free from the pain of the past, where you can grow into the woman you once dreamed about.

Working to heal your inner child can help you resolve some of these issues. Through inner child work, you can treat the wounds you developed as a kid and address your needs that weren't ever met. This can bring up some difficult memories and complicated emotions, so consider doing this work with the help of a licensed therapist. When starting, recognize that your inner child is present within you and that she is hurting. Notice the ways she shows up in your day-to-day life, whether it's the way you people-please and avoid conflict or that constant feeling of inadequacy.

Part of healing your inner child requires some reparenting, so you'll need to listen to what your inner child is saying. She may have been too scared to voice herself before, but she's speaking up now, and you can listen to hear if she's angry, insecure, and/or vulnerable. Communicate with her to help ease some of her anxiety. Consider writing a letter and asking her questions, like how you can best support her. As you're doing this, be sure to treat your inner child well. Think of all the things you wanted to do as a kid but couldn't, whether due to house rules, fear, or money. Do these things now, and take unapologetic joy in them.

Take Your Time with Grief

In the US, when a loved one dies, mourners are given a period of time when bereavement is considered acceptable. Depending on your relationship with the deceased, this span can look like a few days to a few weeks. But ultimately, there is this expectation that at some point, typically when you've used up all your company's allotted bereavement days, you have to pull yourself together and move on. Harsh? This is America, señorita.

But these arbitrary time frames for healing are both ignorant and incredibly insensitive. As those who have lost someone know, grief comes in waves. Some swallow you whole; others you learn to wade through. And like ocean waves, these emotional swells are unpredictable, with ebbs and flows that shift in direction and in intensity. One month you're on autopilot. The next week is filled with panic attacks. Then there comes a day when you feel okay, maybe even normal, until you are hit by yet another overwhelming sweep of salty water. Neither capitalism's rush to return to work nor a cultural discomfort around death can alter the devastating and debilitating whirlpool of grief.

So, amor, this is your permission to mourn for as long as you need to, and to oscillate through all the stages of grief, including the ones that Elisabeth Kübler-Ross, the psychiatrist who developed the model, missed. The process is necessary and it's healthy. So what if it makes someone uncomfortable!

Of course, discomfort is not always the only problem. Many of you might not have the ability to miss weeks or months of work. Maybe you are self-employed, or maybe you have an employer who puts profits over people and cost over compassion. But the response to these difficult realities is not to swallow your grief and pretend you don't feel t. In these moments, it's even more important that you are honest about your emotions and turn to family, friends, and your community for support.

Across Latin America and the Caribbean, there are ancestral practices and r tuals around mourning that recognize and respect this process, many of them rooted in Indigenous and African tradi-tions. In the Dominican Republic, funerals often last nine days: three days of grieving and remembering, three days of silent reverence, and then three days of releasing. In Honduras, there are drumming parties that occur around the anniversary of someone's death, where loved ones gather to eat and drink as drumming is used to elevate the deceased's spirit. And, of course, in Mexico, and now across Latin America, families make elaborate ofrendas for Día de Muertos so that the spirits of departed loved ones can return temporarily. If you're unfamiliar, research how your homeland honors the dead and incorporate it into your own grieving journey.

Phone a Friend for Validation

Feeling your feelings is healthy, pero diablo, it's hard work.

It feels lonely, and at times even embarrassing. Maybe you think you're too smart, too evolved in your healing, to be struggling with the same feelings over and over again. Or perhaps you think the world wouldn't respect you or take you seriously if you were honest about how you feel. You don't give yourself grace with your emotions because you've witnessed how women who look or sound like you are treated when they express their feelings: Latinas lose their jobs for being "too fiery," and our communities discard us as "locas."

But you can't be silent about your pain. If you are struggling with heartache, anger, or confusion, you need to externalize your complex feelings. You can do this by expressing your emotions to the people you trust, folks who are genuinely invested in your well-being: your amiguis.

According to psychotherapist and author Oludara Adeeyo, before you hit up your friends, you should think about what it is you need at the moment: Are you interested in advice or do you simply want to be heard and validated? Next, reach out to the person in your contact list who you think is best equipped to provide this for you right now. When you do, you'll first want to ask if they have the capacity for the conversation. If not, they love you no less—it's just not a good time for them to help right now. Move on to someone else who might have that time and space.

When you find someone who is available to listen to you, let them know what you need and what you're not looking for. When the conversation is over, thank them.

And then, when it's just you, thank yourself for choosing to do right by you in a world that wants you to suffer alone.

Whether the problem you are experiencing is resolved by the phone call or not, simply sharing it helps you to better move through the pain and to be supported by people who love you.

Feel All Your Emotions

On any given day, you can experience a roller coaster of emotions. You can feel joy waking up to the face of someone you love and then get anxious on the way to work because you're running late. Seeing a rainbow before walking into the office can leave you with a sense of awe that is soon replaced by fear when you realize you have to give a presentation. While many emotions feel manageable, others can be overwhelming, prompting you to tuck them away somewhere deep inside where you can return to deal with them another day or, well, never.

This is how society taught you to treat difficult feelings. Babies cry. Adults suck it up. But ignoring your feelings only hurts you even more in the end. The brain's attempts to stop you from feeling your emotions end up putting more stress on your mind and your body. This could lead to both psychological distress, like anxiety and depression, and physical conditions, like heart disease, intestinal problems, headaches, and insomnia.

Feeling your feelings—all of them—is necessary and healthy. Activities like physical movement or making art can be safe, productive ways to express feelings of anger, anxiety, or other complex emotions. By mindfully embracing how you are feeling, you give yourself the opportunity to make sense of your emotions, listening to the often-complicated messages they are telling you so that you can give yourself exactly what you need.

Don't Get Caught Up with Bochinche

There are times when you can—and should—stop minding your own business and start making problems. For instance, you can use the privileges you have—whether they be the color of your skin, immigration status, financial income, or position of power—to uplift marginalized communities and attempt to right terrible wrongs. And then there are times when you do just need to mind your own business. You don't need to hear or participate in venomous chisme. That Twitter, or X, beef everyone is talking about? You don't have to read it or ask questions. It has nothing to do with you, and your two cents won't help ameliorate the toxicity of social media politics anyway.

One of the easiest ways to take care of your mental health is by staying out of the trivial squabbles that don't involve you. You don't have to know the who, what, where, when, why, and how details of every matter, and you definitely don't have to give your every opinion. Preciosa, why would you even want to invite someone else's drama into the sanctuary you are creating for yourself? Unfollow las tóxicas, close the apps, and firmly tell the friend trying to give you the tea that it has nothing to do with y'all. Even when your inner averiguada wants to know what fulana did to fulano, resist the urge. Say no and entertain yourself with content that won't leave you feeling conflicted, stressed, or otherwise grossed out by the state of modern-day pettiness.

As my mother would say, los bochincheros no entran. She was talking about the Kingdom of God. I'm referring to the zen state you're after.

Validate Your Resilience Fatigue

Has anyone ever attempted to compliment you on your resilience? Doesn't that feel like such a twisted trait to be commended on? It's like they're saying your ability to take on trauma, violence, and various forms of oppression and inequality is admirable. Like, yeah? I'm drowning, and instead of passing me a life jacket you tell me to strike a pose because I look great flailing my arms around as I cough up water? I don't know, pero like, that's neither comforting nor useful.

So instead, I'm pulling up in my airboat, tugging you out of the river, and giving you some fresh water to drink as I caress your hair because what you need, baby girl, is someone to validate your struggle and your exhaustion.

Resilience fatigue is the extreme tiredness you feel after attempting to be strong, brave, positive, and motivated while facing adversities and tragedies for too damn long. Every time your body responds to stressors, like when you realize you can't pay a bill on time or you watch your community being displaced by gentrification, it goes through a process of allostasis, which is the attempt to regain homeostasis, or a stable equilibrium. But when you experience stressors repeatedly or for long periods, your body experiences an allostatic load that leads to the loss of adaptive plasticity and resilience. This can lead to mental health conditions, like anxiety disorders or depression, as well as physical health issues, like metabolic syndromes, cardiac diseases, or infection.

While you might not be able to prevent challenges and interruptions to your day-to-day life, you can improve your methods for coping with them. First, set some priorities (but for real this time!)

and give each task an allotted time. Give attention to what absolutely needs to be done and handle what can wait (like the laundry and the dishes) when you're able to. Next, find a simpler method. *Temporarily* tuck the pile of clothes under your bed and use paper plates. Mami doesn't need to know. Finally, release yourself from the guilt. You are prioritizing yourself, your rest, and your future. Those stinky clothes ain't gonna hurt nobody, so release yourself from that negative self-talk.

Set Boundaries
and Honor Them

Latinas bear heavy loads. From work and school to home life and relationships, you might think that you have to do it all and be great—no, perfect—at each task. You have to be the smartest in the classroom, the most innovative in the boardroom, the freakiest in the bedroom, and the most committed in the community. In the end, you end up stretching yourself thin because of this internalized supermujer syndrome, causing low self-esteem, irritability, stress, and anxiety. It ain't worth it, mama.

To avoid getting lost in your work, relationships, and obligations, and to steer clear of being exploited by people who don't really care about your well-being, you must set boundaries. It's how you build agency and personal autonomy.

You can set boundaries in all aspects of your life: physical, sexual, mental, emotional, and financial. Boundaries allow you to decide how you want and don't want to be touched and spoken to. They put you in control over how you spend your money and your time. And you choose how you want to engage (or disengage) with someone who doesn't respect your boundaries.

To set boundaries, you first need to self-reflect. Consider the people and activities that invigorate and/or value you, as well as the ones that leave you feeling exhausted and unappreciated. On a sheet of paper, draw a vertical line. On the left side of the line, write down everything that makes you feel good. On the right side, list what makes you uncomfortable or unhappy. Use this list to decide how you will set boundaries. For example, limit the time you spend doing what's on the right side of the list or, if feasible, eliminate it altogether.

Next, communicate your boundaries to the people in your life. Clearly state your wants and needs so that they are not crossed and you are not taken advantage of.

Finally, and most importantly, uphold your boundaries. This is probably the hardest part because it's so easy to return to people-pleasing patterns. While it's important to be flexible when necessary, reiterating and maintaining boundaries is how you continue to do right by yourself.

Stop Making Yourself Smaller

Latinas are taught to be humble, to not take up too much space, and, above all, to avoid causing a scene. If you're undocumented or grew up in a mixed-status home, keeping your head down is a matter of safety. But under a culture of marianismo, this passivity and silence are considered characteristics of good girls, of pretty girls even. This message is reinforced through the popular and terribly sexist saying: "Calladita te ves más bonita." As a Latina, you've been taught that your womanhood, beauty, and value are often tied to how small you can make yourself, and it's hurting you. In fact, a study published in the *International Journal of Social Psychiatry* found that women who self-silence are more likely to experience physical and mental illnesses like depression and eating disorders, two conditions that Latinas, in particular, experience at equal or higher rates than non-Latine white women (according to *US News & World Report*).

But maybe you've been playing small for so long that you don't even realize when you're doing it. You don't recognize that by playing small, you self-sabotage, undermining your career and your relationships. Playing small can look like staying silent when you have something brilliant to say, not celebrating your wins, and apologizing for your joy and accomplishments. Playing small is hiding in the back of the room where you hope and pray no one will see you, not applying for the job or fellowship you are more than qualified for, and avoiding sharing your talents and wisdom on social media. Pero, mami, I want to see you, hear you, and big you up! Your voice is so essential. Your talents are inspiring. And your story is affirming. You need to know that.

To stop playing small, you need to recognize all the moments when you engage in this behavior. To start, jot down the times you remember silencing yourself and minimizing what you bring to the table. Keep this list handy, because you will add to it as these moments arise again. (Don't feel bad about that, either. Change takes time.) Look over all the examples you cataloged and think about moments when you'll soon be in a similar situation. Make a commitment to yourself to do one thing differently, like sitting at the front of class, sharing your idea in a work meeting, or simply saying thank you rather than deflecting a compliment. Start with simple, easy steps, gradually working your way to a place where you're comfortable being your full, radiant self in every space you occupy.

Let Go of
Impostor Syndrome

There has probably been a time (or many times) when you were the first, the only, or one of a few Latinas to be in certain rooms. Maybe you were the first Latina valedictorian at your high school, the only Latina in your college's STEM program, or one of just two Latinas slated to speak at a conference. Maybe you are in a field where you've never seen others like you, not in reality or on the TV screen. Being the first or the only isn't just lonely; it's intimidating and can make you feel like you don't have enough experience, talent, or smarts to be there—even if your resume and performance offer contradictory evidence.

Impostor syndrome is loosely defined as feeling like a fraud and doubting your skills or abilities. It disproportionately affects high-achieving people and those who have not historically seen themselves in the roles they are presently navigating. As a Latina who may battle perfectionism, supermujer syndrome, and being the first and/or only one in spaces, you are particularly vulnerable to impostor syndrome. In fact, multiple studies have found that Latinas experience impostor syndrome more often than non-Latine white women.

But don't get it twisted, mami; your feelings of self-doubt aren't entirely on you. In fact, these feelings are exacerbated by the historical (and continued) bias and exclusion of racial, ethnic, and class minorities in these spaces. Your gender, ethnicity, and race can oftentimes place you in a precarious position at work, experiencing implicit and explicit biases, stereotypes, and workplace harassment. If you feel inadequate, it could stem from these real-life experiences.

For many people, impostor syndrome doesn't go away with time, experience, or success; however, there are healthy coping mechanisms that can help you externalize these feelings and work through them so that you're able to continue being the jeva that you are. To help combat impostor syndrome, it's important to be connected to people who understand. If you don't feel like you can lean on your friends and family, try a campus organization, employee resource group, professional association, or even a social media community (there are amazing Facebook Groups and Instagram communities dedicated to Latinas across various educational and career fields). These communities will help you realize that you're not alone, provide safe spaces for you to vent, and better equip you to deal with impostor syndrome and the systemic inequalities it's rooted in.

Say No

Latinas say yes a lot, whether it's mami making time in her crammed schedule to meal-prep for you when you're sick or injured, or your own tendency to say yes to another work project when you're already juggling too much at the office. Latinas have this eagerness to please and this urgency to accept any and all proposals. There's also a cultural expectation that women be agreeable and of service. It doesn't matter if it doesn't serve you or, worse, has the potential to cause you stress. While it's beautiful to support loved ones and welcome the universe's blessings, self-care means you have to set boundaries that may, from time to time, require you to say...no.

In the past, you may have felt guilty for saying no to someone or regret for passing on what seemed like a good thing. But think about how you felt when you said yes to something you wanted to say no to: angry, drained, resentful. How can you win? The answer: by knowing what it is that you do and don't want and getting comfortable honoring it.

To start, ask yourself what you want. What do you want to do? How do you want to feel? How do you want to show up for yourself and your loved ones? Compile your answers into a list. Then, when someone asks you for something, return to that list and decide if it's something you actually want to put your time into. If not, say no. No is a complete sentence. You don't owe anyone an explanation, but you can give one if you'd like. The more you say no, the more you honor yourself. And the more you cater to your own wants and needs, the more you build your own sense of self-worth.

Be Flexible and Open to Change

As a Latina, you know that change is constant. Since you or your family migrated, a lot has altered: new laws and norms, different languages and cultures, and, of course, being categorized by the previously unused ethnic label "Latina." Whether you realize it or not, you spend much of your day changing your manners and behaviors depending on who you're around, leaping from one language to another, and reconciling the competing values your ethnic culture places on community and your national culture sets on individualism.

And yet, a lifetime centered on cross-cultural adjustments hasn't made you a change enthusiast. Maybe you're tired of always having to code-switch or alter your plans because of something that's out of your control. To quote Edward James Olmos as Abraham Quintanilla in the 1997 film *Selena*, "It's exhausting!" You want, just for once, some routine that offers you stability and certainty. But while daily regimens can be immensely helpful, you can't live every day crossing off the same checklist. Life be lifing, and allowing yourself to be flexible is how you survive uncomfortable changes.

How can you be flexible? As my Cuban therapist tells me, be like a palm tree. As gusty weather pulls other perennial plants from the ground, these tropical palms usually stay standing. Sure, the trunk might sway violently with the wind, scattering its vibrant leaves along flooded grounds, but the flexibility of these trees allows them to survive severe storms. Embracing change doesn't mean setting an unrealistic expectation for yourself to smile through unplanned hardships and growing pains; it means being as resilient as una palmera, because, hermana, fluidity, adaptability, and malleability are how your people and your land have always persevered.

Ignore the Mean Girl in Your Head

You have a voice in your head. And a lot of the time, that voice is kind of a mean girl. She shows up when you're alone in bed at night and during your job interview. A fast-talker, in seconds she tells you stories about your unworthiness, inexperience, and unpreparedness. And before you're able to mandarla pa'l carajo, her convincing chatter has left you tormented and defenseless.

You're not alone. Most people spend one-third of their lives not living in the present. Instead, they're engaging with that voice in their head: imagining, remembering, and reflecting. This isn't inherently bad. Deliberate self-reflection can be incredibly helpful, and sometimes nostalgia allows you to relive some of the most exciting moments from your past. Unfortunately, chatter, those cyclical negative thoughts that turn a neutral experience like introspection into anxiety and self-sabotage, is often louder than the fun stuff. And the worst part: When you're stressed or the stakes are high, that inner mean girl gets loud like Jennifer Lopez at Joe Biden's presidential inauguration.

Here's the better news: You can quiet your inner mean girl and turn this voice in your head from foe to friend. Your inner voice is a basic feature of the mind. You don't want it to go away. Instead, you want to figure out how to use it more effectively. To introduce more healthy self-talk to your inner dialogue, first identify what your negative chatter sounds like. What are the messages it wants you to believe about yourself or the scenarios you are in? What tends to trigger this mean girl? Next, figure out where this negativity is coming from. Whether through journaling or speaking with a therapist, determine what experiences led you to start talking to yourself so unkindly.

This admittedly not-so-easy work will help you spot chatter as soon as—or even before—it arrives, signaling you to pull out your tools and combat the noise. Your tools can include imagining yourself advising a friend experiencing the same problem as you, reframing the experience as a challenge (one you may have previously already succeeded in), or viewing yourself as a neutral third party. When the voice in your head starts working with you, not against you, you'll have a strong new ally for facing the challenges of life.

Heal or Sever
Complicated Relationships

Being in community with other people is essential to your well-being, but maintaining relationships is complicated. While squabbles are painful, they aren't inherently unhealthy. Really, most relationships, including those with your parents, best friends, primas, or romantic partners, will experience a healthful dose of disagreements and challenges. Other times, relationships can be destructive, especially when there is a history of abuse, manipulation, and lies. Prioritizing your well-being means you'll have to assess your relationships to discern which ones are worth restoring and which ones you need to sever.

As a Latina, you navigate multiple worlds. Inevitably, you learn and grow in and from each of these spaces, and sometimes your changes are confusing to the people you love. Perhaps you start practicing a new religion or embrace a different sexual orientation or gender identity. Oftentimes, this misunderstanding leads to conflict, causing ruptures in your nearest and dearest relationships. Sound familiar? If so, then you know how this antagonism and estrangement can disrupt your day-to-day life, causing intense feelings of shame, guilt, and pain, making it difficult to focus on other tasks, and obstructing your ability to build other relationships. If you believe it's a relationship worth restoring, all parties can work through the obstacles, help heal hurt, and repair the partnership together. Whether you're sitting down for a one-on-one or signing up for couples or group therapy, be mindful of the following:

- *Manage expectations.*
- *Avoid playing the blame game.*
- *Take responsibility for your actions.*

- *Be transparent.*
- *Stay respectful and compassionate.*
- *Learn to compromise.*

But, again, not all relationships are worth reconciling. Sometimes, people straight up don't deserve to be in your life. This doesn't mean they're innately bad people. But if their presence is toxic to your mental health, then cutting them off is what you must do to honor your self-care journey. If you're used to giving people second, third, and more chances, even after they've revealed themselves as unkind to you, allow me to be El Chacal de la Trompeta and yell "y...¡fuera!" to the folks who have to go: the abusive, gaslighting, manipulative, and controlling; the boundary crossers; the liars; the narcissists; the judgmental ones; those who take but don't give; and, of course, la gente que te deja drenada.

When you're ready to sever the relationship, release yourself from the guilt. Know that they are responsible for both the actions that got them cut from your life and the emotions they may use to attempt to manipulate you into giving them another chance. Not this time. If you're going to explain your breakup, do so in a public setting where you feel safe, or consider writing them a letter. Also, respect your own boundaries. If it's helpful, block their number and their social media so that you are not tempted to reach out to them.

Finally, release yourself from the trauma or pain of that relationship. You might be able to do this with a cord-cutting ritual (a spiritual process of releasing yourself from people, situations, or beliefs), or you may benefit from therapy. Do whatever it is that you need to do.

Stop Judging Yourself

You know that really judgmental tía, abuela, or comadre, the one you're very careful about what you say in front of and are uncomfortable being unkempt around because she will deliver a whole unwarranted sermon for you? Y'all are more alike than you think you are. The difference: She spends her time assessing everyone around her, while you, my love, judge everything about yourself.

Maybe you judge yourself because you're not where you thought you would be at this stage in your life. Maybe it's because the shape of your body has changed (which is very normal, by the way). Perhaps it's because you're a bilingual mami and used the wrong English word during your work presentation. Or maybe it's because you messed up, pretty badly, and you can't seem to forgive yourself.

You're going to let yourself, and others, down every once in a while. You're going to do something cringe many times in your life. Así es la vida. You're a human being with a full range of emotions who makes mistakes. Sometimes gaffes will happen in front of an audience or you will unintentionally (or intentionally) hurt someone else. Being overly self-critical isn't going to change this about yourself. Being self-judgmental isn't going to absolve you from the pain you may have caused. No, it only leads to more harm—including mental health conditions, like anxiety and depression, or substance abuse—to yourself and, potentially consequently, those around you.

To stop judging yourself, first notice *when* you're judging yourself. Words like "should" are a pretty big giveaway. Next, determine where your judgments are coming from. Through journaling or meditation, ask yourself a few questions: Do these judgments echo what others have said about you, including family, ex-partners, or society? Are they rooted in pain you caused someone else? If the former, take inventory of those who have introduced these toxins into your psyche and consider setting boundaries with them. If the latter, apologize and make amends to the person you hurt. Whether they accept your apology or not, you will need to forgive yourself and stop judging your present self for something your former self did.

Next, start getting comfortable with your emotions, including the favorable and not-so-favorable ones. Feeling all of your emotions is healthy, so try not to judge yourself for having human reactions. Instead, recognize that your emotions exist for a reason, and they may be trying to tell you something.

Finally, try to look at the situation as an outsider and treat yourself as you would a friend. Even if they messed up, you wouldn't kick them when they're down. No, you'd keep it real while being nonjudgmental and encouraging. Show that same love and acceptance to yourself.

Trust Yourself

Latinas have long been categorized as untrustworthy. Sexism, xeno-phobia, racism, and classism coalesce to create stereotypes like the deceptive femme fatale, the criminal hyperfertile mother of "anchor babies," and the confused elder que "no espeake inglés." Even when you don't want to, it's easy to internalize the message behind many of these tropes: You are not a reliable source, even when the subject is your own life.

Pero, mami, this changes now. There is no one more import-ant to trust than yourself. When you have low self-trust, you're constantly second-guessing your experiences and skills, you're so scared to make the wrong decision that you don't make one at all, and you're susceptible to others gaslighting you and taking advan-tage of you. But when you are confident in yourself, your offerings, and your decisions, you gracefully and optimistically move in ways that serve and honor you and your truth.

To start, understand what self-trust looks like: being aware of your thoughts, feelings, and needs; expressing them without shame; sticking to your core values; and following your passions. You can start practicing self-trust by being kinder to yourself. This means speaking back to the internal chatter when it tells you you're not good enough to pursue what you want and giving yourself the per-mission (and pep talk) to go after it. It's all about being and express-ing your authentic self, which may require you to be vulnerable and set boundaries with people who feel uncomfortable watching you take charge of your life.

Journal to Process Your Feelings

The amount of things you have to deal with on any given day as a woman, and a Latina, is wild. From street harassment, to state-sanctioned intimidation, to microaggressions, life can feel like an Amanda Serrano vs. Erika Cruz boxing match, with challenging situations thrown your way left and right. You encounter an array of potentially traumatic or frightening experiences each time you leave your home—and for some, even your place of residence isn't safe.

To process all of the thoughts, feelings, and experiences that occur during your day, try writing in a journal. Journaling has been proven to help improve mental health, encourage self-confidence, boost emotional intelligence, inspire creativity, and achieve goals. This is because when you write about the good, the bad, and the complicated of your day, you allow yourself to understand how you feel about what's happening around you and process and external-ize those emotions. Journaling can lead to transformative break-throughs and healing.

There's no one way to journal. You can incorporate it into a daily, weekly, monthly, or quarterly routine, or you can write when-ever you're called to do so. In the morning, you can write about last night's dreams. And at night, you can scribe about the day. You can journal about your career goals, relationships, or something you're working through in therapy. You can write about what you're grate-ful for and return to the pages for beautiful reminders of all the ways you're loved and supported when life gets complicated again. You can purchase a journal that already comes with prompts to guide you in your self-awareness or healing, or you can write in the notes app on your phone. There are no rules; just write.

Take a Social Media Break

Social media can be a beautiful space to build community—and it can also be frighteningly toxic. Searching "Latina" on just about every social networking app populates images, videos, and comments that reduce Latinas to objects to be consumed, sexualized, critiqued, and discarded, oftentimes without anyone's consent.

But you don't have to search keywords for your newsfeed to disrupt your day. Even if you follow friends, like-minded creators, and otherwise positive content, you'll undoubtedly find yourself tapping through triggering stories of violence against marginalized communities or comparing yourself to the highly curated lives of those you follow. Inevitably, you close the app feeling worse than you did when you opened it.

If social media drains you more than it feeds you, it's time for a break. Regardless of how long a break you take, you will experience the benefits. It frees you from the pressure to perform—and the stress, anxiety, and embarrassment that often accompany this public performance. Without the glamorously packaged pics of people's lives on your smartphone screen, you're less likely to compare your real life to others' staged realities. And most importantly, you will begin to remember that your self-worth isn't tied to likes or views.

Consider moving social media apps on your phone to spots where you can't easily see them, or temporarily delete them altogether. This change doesn't have to be forever. Decide how long you will be off the apps. If your income depends on your social presence, take a shorter break or schedule posts that publish automatically. Finally, track how you feel when you step away from the screen to determine if it's worth making more long-term adjustments.

Stop Consuming Media That Makes You Feel Bad about Yourself

It's wild how unapologetic people are in their hate. Everywhere you look, the suffering and oppression of Latines, and other marginalized communities, are on display. From headline-making images of Border Patrol agents on horseback attempting to whip Haitian migrants and political commentators referring to Latines as dangerous criminals, to films that hinge on Latine trauma and shows that reproduce troubling stereotypes, it's difficult to not be triggered every time you're trying to stay informed or simply enjoy some entertainment.

So, mami, when you need to, just stop. You can stay up-to-date about matters that are important to you and your folks without tuning into the twenty-four-hour news cycle. Change the channel and mute that shawty you've been following on Twitter/X or Instagram if you need a break from videos about anti-Black and anti-trans violence. Temporarily pause the newsletter that updates you on anti-immigration legislation or shares stories about how people who look like you were forced to carry a pregnancy to term against their will. Also, skip that new, trending streaming series that centers your affliction. You can see yourself represented on-screen without sickening your mind. Why inflict pain on yourself in this way, love? Why make your day harder to get through?

Instead, consume media that makes you feel good about yourself. No, there aren't many films and TV series that reflect the diversity, joy, humor, romance, or nuance of Latine communities, but if you ask your friends for recs or follow creatives whose work you respect, you'll find those projects you can kick back and revel in with your bag of Takis like you deserve.

End the Cycle of Generational Trauma

When your trauma is unresolved, it's often passed down to your progeny in a cycle that is called intergenerational trauma. Since mental healthcare has historically been inaccessible and stigmatized among Latine communities, Latinas are particularly vulnerable to intergenerational trauma.

Many Latine families continue to reel, often unconsciously, from the legacies of colonialism and political violence in their home countries, the complicated process of migration, and the othering and violence that is often experienced in their new country. For Latinas who are Black, Indigenous, and/or Asian, this trauma can be compounded by a history of enslavement, genocide, and rape.

This emotional, psychological, or even genetic wounding can be passed down in several ways, including parenting styles and family dynamics, and can increase the risk of mental health issues, substance abuse, and relationship difficulties. When this trauma stays untreated and the cycles proceed unchallenged, the effects inform everything about how someone moves through the world, deepening generational poverty, unstable living environments, and compromised parenting.

To break the cycle of generational trauma, understand how it manifests in your own life:

- *What are the triggers for you?*
- *How have these triggers previously incited you?*

Next, recognize any patterns or attitudes from your family that might show up in how you react to those triggers. Throughout this process, be compassionate with yourself as well as your loved ones, who likely also inherited this trauma from their ancestors.

Finally, get help. Consider working with a licensed therapist and/or reading books like Mariel Buqué's *Break the Cycle: A Guide to Healing Intergenerational Trauma*. Healing intergenerational trauma is complicated, challenging, and may bring up experiences and feelings you don't know how to work through. It takes time and care, but breaking the chains of generational trauma is worth it. It gives you and your progeny freedom.

Don't Internalize Stereotypes

Sometimes it seems impossible to feel good about yourself when so much of what you've been taught about who you are is steeped in adverse stereotypes.

Stereotypes are usually thought about as simple, preconceived ideas people have about others based on their race, ethnicity, gender, immigration status, ability, sexual orientation, or other social identities. These contrived generalizations are often internalized, causing people to have negative preconceptions about themselves and their abilities. For instance, as a Latina, you've been taught by the dominant culture that women like you are inferior, lazy, and unintelligent; as a result, you may tell yourself you can't attain a doctoral degree, that you're not ready to apply for the job you want, or that you'll never be able to buy a house. And these internalized biases end up stopping you from applying for the academic program, that job, or a home loan.

To unlearn internalized biases, first identify the stereotypes you have about yourself and other Latina women. If it's helpful, write them down. Next, figure out where you learned them: Were they taught to you by pop culture, your education system, or perhaps a relative who is also, maybe unknowingly, struggling with internalized biases? Next, investigate why such stereotypes were generated in the first place, looking into the history of colonialism, racism, sexism, xenophobia, or transphobia that led to their propagation and perpetuation. Consider who benefits and who is harmed by your internalization of these biases. Finally, if you need further support, seek therapy and/or networks of unfettered Latinas to learn from and get inspired by.

Embrace Nuance

Social media has a lot of people thinking in chasms. Dangerous diet fads that go viral on these apps command users to cut carbs or pile them on, leaving no room for people to trust their bodies and eat intuitively. Meanwhile, news headlines spin faster than Iris Chacón, with thousands of people sharing and commenting about stories they never clicked to read, misinterpreting and misinforming their followers about the news they promote or criticize.

In some ways, it's understandable; in fact, it's how the brain operates. When you're perplexed or overwhelmed, say by the stress of what it means to exist as a Latina in your society and the precariousness of the world for marginalized communities, your brain looks for greater simplicity and clarity, not more complexity. Logic and analysis are higher-level mental functions that are too arduous for a stressed brain, so your mind is more susceptible to black-and-white thinking, even if the beliefs are incomplete, irrational, or illogical.

But few things are ever dichotomous, amor. Your life, your experiences, your relationships, your desires, and your cultures—like everyone's—are complex. Embracing nuance ensures you're never placed in a limiting box. Welcoming nuance means being suspicious of binaries and binary thinking that could lead to oversimplifying complex people, communities, experiences, and information. Nuance will allow you to think beyond whether things are "good" or "bad" or "right" or "wrong" so that you can make decisions that serve the wholeness of you.

Do a Grounding Practice That Works for You

Life can be so overwhelming. There are the demands of work and home, and for you, amor, there are also microaggressions, videos of Latine youth locked up in cages, and clashing cultural expectations. The need to perform, to keep moving, even while you feel like you are falling apart, can lead to debilitating anxiety attacks. It can leave you restless, sick, or in a state of numbing terror. When this happens, it feels as if there is no return to normalcy, to lucidity, to safety. But there is, and grounding practices are what will bring you back to the present moment.

A grounding practice is an exercise that helps you focus on the present moment so that you are able to distract yourself from enervating flashbacks or anxiety peaks. These exercises require you to use some or all of your senses to move through the distress. There are numerous types of grounding practices, and some that work for others may or may not work for you. So you, preciosa, will have to uncover which exercises help you.

There are physical, mental, and soothing grounding exercises. Physical exercises include focusing on the breath; moving your body through a short walk; performing an action in place, like jumping jacks; or savoring a scent, food, or drink. Another physical exercise is the 5-4-3-2-1 method, which encourages you to list specific quantities of different items you hear, see, touch smell, and taste. Mental grounding exercises include reciting a mantra or song, using an anchoring phrase, visualizing yourself doing a task you enjoy, or playing a memory game. Finally, soothing exercises can include imagining the face or voice of someone you love, embracing a pet, listening to meditative music or sounds, or indulging in something physically comforting, like taking a warm bath, touching a sweater, or covering yourself with a weighted blanket.

Remember: The aim of the grounding practice is to distract yourself from whatever is causing you distress by bringing you back into the present moment where you can regain control of your thoughts and emotions. This activity can be unique to you, but it's important to adopt one, or some, that can be used whenever and wherever you're at.

Join a Support Group

While mental health conditions don't discriminate, media aimed at destigmatizing psychiatric disorders and therapy still tend to look one way: young, upper middle class, and non-Latine white. The absence of people who look or sound like you in film, TV, or awareness campaigns can make the experience of looking for help feel all the more isolating. But support groups can help you see that you're not in this alone.

A support group provides people who are going through, or have gone through, similar experiences an opportunity to connect with each other, providing an open space to share feelings, occurrences, insight, and aid. There are support groups for just about any concern or condition, including eating disorders, substance abuse, grief, anxiety, depression, and bipolar disorder, to name a few. Whether facilitated by a licensed mental health professional or peer-led, these spaces offer emotional support, understanding and affirmation, encouragement, and community.

Although most support groups, which are usually more affordable than other mental health treatment, can help you learn more about your condition, reduce distress, and normalize what you're going through, a support space that is by and for Latinas, or women from marginalized racial or ethnic communities more generally, may feel like a safer space for you to share, release, and heal. And thanks to the Internet, these communities are more accessible than ever before. Various accredited mental health associations, organizations, and platforms provide virtual support groups for women and People of Color, including some by and for Latinas specifically, that are free, low-cost, or use a sliding scale fee model.

Find a Latina Therapist

While Latinas aren't a monolith, there are certain shared cultural experiences, traditions, and expectations. Many would have to be explained to someone who doesn't come from a similar cultural background, and some, even when clarified, could still leave folks a little confused. This is why having a therapist who looks like you or shares a similar background to you is essential to your mental health.

Licensed mental health professionals provide empathic listening, evaluate your needs, and offer care that facilitates your growth or treats mental or emotional disorders. It's work that is complicated, heavy, and may require you to invest money and time. Working with someone with a similar background allows you to show up as your whole self without having to explain critical aspects of your cultural or racial identities, allows you to express yourself bilingually, and may decrease your risk of being misdiagnosed.

In fact, Latinas are more likely to be misdiagnosed for psychotic disorders. Oftentimes, it's because culturally normative behaviors are mistaken for psychopathology. For instance, many Latine cultures and spiritual practices engage with the deceased. A non-Latina therapist might view these traditions and rituals as indicators of a mental health disorder, but a Latina licensed professional may be able to distinguish between these ancestral practices and psychiatric disorders.

Working with a Latina therapist could be affirming and transformative. And with online directories like Latinx Therapy, it's easier to find licensed mental health professionals near you. Of course, just because a therapist is Latina doesn't mean it's going to be a great fit. Know that it's okay to date around before committing to a therapist you like.

part two
Body

It's not vain to care for your body. For Latinas, it's absolutely essential. Trauma is stored in your muscles, and daily stressors weaken your immune system. Left unprocessed, these wounds manifest as physical aches and illnesses that can turn chronic and even fatal. This is why learning to listen to the messages your body is communicating to you and proactively taking care of your physical health are acts of radical self-care.

But to properly tend to your body you first have to believe it's worthy of care. Society has repeatedly taught you as a Latina that your body is less valuable. Throughout history, the Latina body has been pillaged and discarded. It's been forced to measure its worthiness against a Eurocentric beauty standard that is unrealistic to most. And it's been denied humane healthcare.

In this section, you'll find exercises that will help you heal your relationship with your body and show you how to care for it. Some actions might not be accessible to you depending on your physical abilities, but there will be many others you can do. There are practices that will teach you how to reconnect with your body and how to nourish and advocate for your physical and sexual health. This is what bodily care looks like.

Dance to Release Trauma

According to a 2022 report by the American Psychological Association, Latinas are more likely to experience stress related to violence than any other ethnic or racial group. Whether tied to sexual or physical abuse, gun violence, or state-sanctioned brutality, this trauma is stored in the body, causing your nervous system to stay on high alert and leaving you susceptible to chronic pain, chest tightness, insomnia, brain fog, and dissociation. As harrowing as this truth is, there is something you can do: dance.

Dancing is an easy and joyous way to release trauma and reconnect with your body. It supports cardiovascular health, strengthens your muscles, improves balance, and boosts cognitive performance. Add a little merengue típico to the mix and it's a pari that your spirit can revel in as well! Similarly, sensual dance, like pole, samba, and perreo, can help you reconnect with your body and your sexuality, heal old wounds, and elevate your self-esteem.

To start incorporating more dance into your lifestyle, turn up the volume on your favorite songs and dance alone in the comfort of your home. You can move your hips intuitively while cooking a meal or practice your footwork by following along to a YouTube tutorial. If you want to dance in community, host home parties and play your favorite salsa, cumbia, and vallenato classics with your loved ones; schedule monthly nights out at clubs, bars, or restaurants that play music genres you enjoy; or join a Latine dance class. If you're doing the latter, find classes taught by Latines. There's something troubling about all the non-Latine white folks making money teaching styles of movement that Latines were once derided for enjoying. Regardless, just dip it low and pick it up slow like Christina Milian taught you.

Ask for a Hug (or Hug Yourself)

There's something divine about a consensual hug. It can bond you with another or make you feel comforted and loved. And this is because there is real healing power in human touch. When you give or receive a welcomed hug, your body releases a delicious sancocho of feel-good hormones like dopamine, serotonin, and oxytocin. Dopamine induces feelings of pleasure, serotonin makes you happy, and oxytocin fills your body with sensations of love. It's exquisite.

Unfortunately, many Latinas, especially those who live far away from loved ones, work remotely, or otherwise feel alone in their professional and personal lives, are starving for touch. This is especially true for the supermujer, that Latina who sacrifices herself, including her desire for romantic and platonic relationships, to excel in every other aspect of her life. But, amorcita, without physical affection, you can experience loneliness, depression, attachment issues, poor sleep quality, or even difficulty feeling emotions at all.

To experience the warm, healthful benefits of a hug, find someone you love or trust to hold you. You can have a cuddle sesh with your darling, amiguis, sister, baby, niece, tía, parent, or pet. Or you can ask that kind colleague or neighbor, the caring acquaintance you don't have an intimate relationship with but know would embrace you without pity or suspicion, for a needed hug. Maybe it becomes the way you greet and depart from your folks. Or maybe, when you're alone at night, it's how you hold and caress yourself. Regardless of whose body you hug, yours or someone else's, this gentle embrace will make you feel comforted and cared for.

Get a Massage

Hermosa, you need a massage. Yes, you. As a Latina, you've been taught to move through life as a supermujer, saving the day, your community, and your coins, all while ignoring the aches, stress, and tension in your body prompted by your acts of service. That's not sustainable. You need to serve yourself, too, and one of the most nourishing ways to treat your cuerpo is with a massage.

By rubbing and kneading the skin, muscles, tendons, and ligaments, massages help reduce pain and tightness in your body, kindle relaxation, strengthen your immune system, and ease stress. It's reinvigorating.

Once upon a time, this integrative medicine was only available to the wealthy at exclusive spas, but now massages are accessible to nearly everyone. If you have the financial means, consider booking monthly or seasonal massages at a local parlor. Or bring the rubdowns home by buying a handheld massager that you can use as little or as often as you'd like. But a massage doesn't have to cost you anything. If you live with someone—a romantic partner, a parent, or a friend—ask them to massage your back, neck, and shoulders. If you live alone, consider adding thigh, leg, and foot massages to your bedtime routine. All you need to do is commit to regularly kneading out the tension in your muscles to provide your body with the relief and relaxation it deserves.

Stretch Every Morning

Are you stretching, beba? Stretching por la mañana helps your body gradually wake up, moving you from relaxed to energized. When you gently stretch your neck, back, legs, and feet, your body produces serotonin, which reduces stress and increases vitality. By stretching in the morning, you minimize pain, boost circulation, and power yourself to get through the day.

To get started, check with your doctor to be sure a stretching routine will work for you. Carve out a few minutes in your morning routine to stretch. You can start while in bed, performing a knee to chest stretch:

While lying on your back with one leg extended, hug the bent knee of the other leg into your chest, pulling down gently. Move your knee in small circles, first in one direction, then the other. Next squeeze your knee to your chest for thirty seconds, then switch legs and move to the other side.

Still not quite ready to get out of bed? Try a lying spinal twist stretch:

While lying on your back, bend both knees into your chest, hugging your legs gently. Release your arms into a T position. Keeping your spine flat, allow your knees to fall to the left side. Don't worry if your legs can't move very far at first. Pause for a few breaths, then move your knees to the right side. Pause for a few breaths, then bring your legs back to center and release.

If you have more time, consider introducing a yoga practice into your morning routine. You can take an in-person yoga class or you can follow along to a free, beginner-friendly lesson like those offered by Tejana instructor Adriene Mishler on her YouTube channel, Yoga with Adriene.

85

Learn to Listen to What Your Body Is Communicating to You

Amor, how many times have you felt exhausted but carried on? Your feet could barely hold you up and your tiredness was dizzying, but you still worked and went out for drinks afterward. Maybe you had to pee, but you held your knees together until you finished your assignment. Or perhaps your stomach was growling from hunger, but you didn't dine until everyone else in the house was fed, tucked into bed, and your kitchen was Fabuloso clean. Your body is communicating with you. It knows what it needs, and it's begging you for it. But can you understand what it's telling you?

Your body is constantly communicating with you. If you've been working out a lot and your muscles are feeling sore, it could be time for a rest day. If you're dizzy or experiencing a headache, you might need a meal or a drink of water. If you feel a lump in your breast, you should book an exam immediately to rule out cancer. And if you notice more facial hair or acne, it could be a sign of polycystic ovary syndrome (PCOS) or endometriosis.

To understand what your body is telling you and what you need to do to support it, pay attention to the sensations you feel throughout your cuerpo at all times: when you are tired *and* rested, sick *and* well, nervous *and* confident, hungry *and* full. This will help you understand what is standard for your body, and knowing that will help you notice when something in your body feels different. One of the easiest and most effective ways to do this is through a body scan. This is a meditation that requires you to focus on different regions of your body so that you can identify how each part feels. Depending on the results of your body scan, you might want to treat that tension or those aches through stretches, massages, or exercise. If the pain is more intense or chronic, it could signal that it's time to visit a primary care physician or specialist.

To perform a body scan, begin by lying down on your bed or on the floor. Next, take a few slow, deep breaths. Pay attention to your breath, noticing as your abdomen expands and contracts. After that, bring your attention to your feet, observing both the sensations you feel and the thoughts or emotions that accompany them. If you feel pain or discomfort, focus your attention on it by breathing into it. When you're ready, move on to your calves, knees, and thighs until you make your way up to the top of your head. Take mental note of wherever you feel pressure, tightness, or pain. Your body has just revealed to you the areas where it needs extra care. Draw on what you've learned about self-care to show it some love.

Find a Doctor Who's Right for You

When was the last time you saw a doctor? Chances are it was too long ago. According to a 2022 Pew Research Center survey, Latinas are less likely than women of any other racial or ethnic group to seek medical care. The reasons are layered: Latinas are less likely to have health insurance. Undocumented Latinas fear receiving medical services because of their status. Many experience language and cultural barriers with medical professionals. And—oh, yeah—it's wildly expensive.

However, when Latinas don't receive the professional healthcare needed, the outcomes are devastating. Latinas are at a greater risk of dying from untreated diabetes, heart disease, breast cancer, cervical cancer, and other diseases. Sometimes, these fatal illnesses can be avoided by seeing a doctor as soon as concerns develop, if not before. When you see a healthcare provider regularly, you learn about health conditions and diseases earlier, improving your chances for getting the proper treatment swiftly and with fewer complications.

So, my love, you're going to need to start seeing a doctor on a consistent basis. You can find a doctor who takes your insurance by contacting your insurance provider and asking for a list of local physicians or by using an online service like Zocdoc. Digital databases like this one also let you know which medical practitioners will see patients without insurance, offer sliding scales or finance plans, and have staff that speak your language. Once you find a doctor, schedule an appointment for a checkup. During your visit, your doctor may order blood tests to check your overall health, so go with an empty stomach. Pro tip: Try to book an early appointment so that you're not hungry throughout the day. When you're there, be honest with your doctor. Don't let shame or embarrassment keep you from sharing vital information or asking questions. If you're uncomfortable speaking up or are unsure what to communicate, bring a friend or relative along who can share your concerns and support you. Be sure to also take notes.

Regardless of the results, you need to understand what your physician is telling you, and you'll want to be able to return to that information to make sound decisions about your health and measure any changes. Before you leave, ask the doctor when you should return and mark that date in your calendar so that you know when you should start scheduling the next appointment. Consistency is critical.

Suck It Up and Do Preventive Tests

According to the Centers for Disease Control and Prevention (CDC), Latinas are less likely than women of every other race and ethnicity to undergo routine preventive screenings. Consequently, Latinas die more often from breast and cervical cancers. Actually, breast cancer is the leading cause of cancer-related deaths among Latinas. Being proactive and scheduling screening tests is an important way to catch any potential issues as early as possible.

For cis Latinas who are twenty-one or older, schedule a Pap test every three years. The procedure is, admittedly, unpleasant, but it's also usually quick. It requires the physician to insert a speculum into the vagina so that they can remove cells to screen for cervical cancer and certain types of human papillomavirus (HPV).

By age forty, both cis and some trans Latinas should begin mammogram screening every year or two depending on your medical history. During these tests, a doctor or lab technician will take an X-ray of your breasts. Again, it can be uncomfortable, but it doesn't take long. Regardless of your age, it's important to conduct monthly self-exams. Begin by lying down on your back. Lift one arm up above your head and use your fingers on the other hand to rub your breast in a circular motion, feeling for any lumps. Repeat these steps with your other breast. If you feel a bump, schedule an appointment with your physician immediately. But don't panic. Your body can also develop noncancerous bumps for different reasons.

Finally, if you're having sex of any kind, make sure you're getting tested for sexually transmitted infections (STIs). The CDC reports that Latines are more likely to contract human immunodeficiency virus (HIV), gonorrhea, and chlamydia. At minimum, you should be screened for syphilis, chlamydia, gonorrhea, and HIV once a year. If you're having sex with multiple partners or with someone who has other partners, get tested every three to six months. But if you're feeling unusual itching, burning, bumps, or discharge, get tested ASAP.

These are some of the most common tests, but ask your doctor what other screenings might be right for you based on your individual health profile.

Start a Bedtime Routine to Improve Your Sleep

Are you tired, ma? It makes sense if you are. A study published in the journal *Social Work in Public Health* found that English-speaking Latines experience more fatigue than Spanish-speaking Latines. And it's not a shocker. The more acculturated you are, the more likely you are to engage in toxic hustle culture, the capitalist expectation that you must grind hard and sacrifice your health and joy to earn more money and climb the career ladder. And for Latinas, who on average earn 31 percent less than non-Latine white women, that ascension is steeper. It's exhausting. You need rest.

Rest is fundamental to every aspect of your life. Taking breaks will allow your body and your mind to recover and refortify. Rest has been proven to reduce stress, lower blood pressure, improve immune health, strengthen the cardiovascular system, ease chronic pain, improve overall mood, sharpen memory and brain function, and contribute to many other health benefits.

To make sure you're getting an appropriate amount of rest, start by getting adequate sleep each night. According to the CDC, adults need at least seven hours of sleep. With so much on your plate, you might require more. Discover how many hours of sleep you need to feel rested and restored and give yourself a bedtime that permits you those hours of zzz's before your alarm goes off.

If you have trouble falling asleep, improve sleep hygiene by creating a bedtime routine. To start, maintain a consistent sleep schedule so that your body begins to learn when it's time to go to bed and wake up. To help you wind down, practice bedtime rituals. Start by turning off your electronic devices and putting away distractions. To encourage relaxation, take a warm bath or shower, make sure the temperature of your room is comfortable, turn on an essential oil diffuser, and/or use a sound machine to play a guided meditation or white noise. If you have a partner who snores, invest in ear plugs. Figure out what relaxes you and keeps you sound asleep throughout the night, and then incorporate these practices into your bedtime routine to ensure you feel rested and restored when you stretch yourself awake the next day.

Cook One of Abuelita's Recipes

Abuelitas prepare meals with love and sabor. In every spoon, there's a taste of home: a faraway land, an unbroken chain of ancestors and descendants, and unreserved love that fills the spirit and the belly. Whether you ever tasted your grandmother's cuisine fresh from the olla or you heard tales of its appetizing and healing properties as someone recreated it, you may have been nourished by her recipes. And one of the most delectable ways to treat your body is to cook one of those special plates yourself.

Your ancestors prepared well-balanced, nutrient-rich dishes sourced from the land for centuries. Across Latin America and the Caribbean, these included stews featuring root vegetables like yuca, yautía, ñame, batata, mapuey, yacón, and maca; plant-based, protein-rich sides of arroz con frijoles or habichuelas; and delectable desserts made out of native fruits like pitaya, açaí, guayaba, mamey, mangó, and camu camu.

Cooking one of abuelita's recipes will nourish your body and satisfy your soul. To start, think of those tasty dishes that comforted you as a kid. Maybe a recipe didn't actually come from your grandmother but, instead, someone else in your family or perhaps even an unrelated loved one whose fare always felt like home. As you're cooking, feel free to make the recipe your own, adjusting it to accommodate your dietary needs. Revel in the sensory-rich experience. Delight in all the colors of the ingredients; savor the aroma of the garlic, onions, or peppers; and dance to the music they make as they fry or boil. Feel the disparate textures of each ingredient, and relish the scrumptious taste of history in every bite.

In addition to reliving tender, loving memories through food, you can create new memories by sharing your abuelita's dishes with others. If you're able to, write these recipes down on paper and describe how each plate makes you feel. Preserve these culinary stories for future generations. Maybe one day, you'll be the abuela (or tía or comadre) that someone else remembers.

Learn Your Cultural Folkloric Dances

Movement has always been a part of your lineage. Your ancestors danced, perhaps as a form of protest, maybe to claim joy, or possibly as a love language. Each Latin American and Caribbean country and territory has its own folkloric forms of movement, and learning these steps and sways could be a mentally and spiritually invigorating way to move your body.

A folk dance is a type of baile that reflects the life of the people of a certain country or region, often at a particular time. In Puerto Rico, bomba is a style of music and dance created by enslaved Africans as a rhythmic conversation and organizing tool to initiate rebellions. In Ecuador, La Caderona is a folkloric dance style and story about the alluring beauty of women of African descent. Meanwhile, punta, a folk dance of the Garínagu, Afro-Indigenous communities in Central America with roots in the Caribbean island of Saint Vincent, represents its peoples' anti-colonial struggles, retention of culture, and celebration of survival.

For Black and Indigenous Latinas, reconnecting with folkloric dances can be medicinal. These dances, which are often a dialogue between the body and the musical instruments, teach you how to be fully embodied, using your hips or shoulders to do the talking. Even more, by carrying on these styles, you connect with your ancestors, each sway sharing a lesson of your history, each spin preserving their existence, and each gyration a reclamation of the freedom, healing, and joy they fought and danced for.

To start, research your cultural folkloric dances. Learn about the different styles, history, and narratives each one shares. Be respectful in your selection, choosing one that is most likely tied to your ancestral history and isn't just part of the national imagination of your origin land. Seek out instructors in your community. You might be surprised by who is working to preserve these folk traditions locally. If you can't find anyone close by, search online. Many instructors provide free video lessons, or online communities can help point you in the best direction.

Adorn Yourself in Your Culture's Traditional Garbs

Cultural or traditional fashion refers to clothing or accessories inspired by one's heritage and upbringing. Throughout history, women in Latin American and Caribbean países adorned their bodies in ways that expressed their identity, culture, and history. Indigenous women in what is now Mexico and Central America wove intricate textiles in color codes that secretly celebrated their ancestors and spiritual practices while under Spanish colonialism. In nineteenth-century Argentina, women in Buenos Aires distanced themselves from Spanish culture by turning the traditional Spanish hair comb into a peinetón, a large, decorative hairpiece that publicized their political support of the ongoing battles for independence.

As your ancestors migrated to other parts of the world, these garbs and accessories were often misunderstood and mocked, prompting a feeling of shame around them. But now, preciosa, you are ready to unlearn the racism and xenophobia and boldly take up space. Reclaiming your traditional styles of dress is one way you can do this. Research traditional clothing from your country of origin and current designers who are inspired by folk styles. Look through old photos or discover period art pieces that can give you a glimpse into former fashion and beauty trends. Talk to the elders in your life about that elaborate scarf, hairpin, or flower crown they've worn for decades.

There is already a growing movement to support Latina-owned brands. And now, you can also adorn your body with pieces inspired by your culture and identity, working these items into your wardrobe and aesthetic in a way that feels authentic to you.

Don't Skip Meals or Count Calories

Have you ever been so busy at work or school that you forget to eat a meal? You need to quit with that, mami. Food powers every system in your body, so when you skip a meal, your whole body, including your mind, is impacted.

Failing to eat nutrient-rich, solid dishes throughout your day—because you forgot, you're calorie counting as part of a diet trend, or you're struggling with other forms of disordered eating—can have serious consequences. Missing out on meals can lower your blood sugar levels, making you feel tired, irritable, confused, and dizzy. Your body may begin to increase production of cortisol, a hormone linked to stress and anxiety. Additionally, missing or severely limiting meals can lead to nutrient deficiencies, which can make you vulnerable to various health conditions, and may cause your digestion to become irregular.

If you have a habit of forgetting to eat because of your daily responsibilities, add breakfast, lunch, dinner, and snack breaks into your planner so that you are notified when that time arrives. Be aware that skipping meals or following calorie-restricted diets can also be linked to disordered eating, and battling disordered eating is not something you can do alone. There are Latina therapists, dietitians, and online support groups sharing tools and resources to help you in your recovery.

Eat More Plantitas

Latinas have a special relationship with plantitas. When you were sick as a kid, maybe your abuelita would walk to her garden to gather some plants and herbs to concoct a remedy. Or perhaps you have distinct memories of watching your mami talk to her house plantas like they were her most treasured amiguis. These practices go back, way back, to when African and Indigenous women across Latin America and the Caribbean became curanderas who used native flora, often illegally under Spanish imperialism, to heal wounds, ease pain, aid rest, and support transformative spiritual experiences for members of their communities. And centuries later, your green thumb or appreciation for the beauty of greenery is, possibly, rooted in this heritage.

Somehow, despite this centuries-long relationship with plants, Latinas still don't eat enough greens. To be fair, most adults, regardless of race and ethnicity, aren't consuming a diet rich in fruits and vegetables. In fact, according to the CDC, only one in ten adults in the US are getting enough plants in their meals. And even though Latinas are actually more likely to eat fruits than other folks, it's still not enough.

Plant-rich diets strengthen your immune system, improve your heart health, reduce the risk of cognitive impairment, and increase your life span. A healthy diet is especially necessary for Latinas, who tend to have more risk factors for cardiovascular disease and are more likely to develop Alzheimer's disease or other dementias.

To get more plants onto your plate, start by eating the vegetables, herbs, and fruits you grew up with so that you really enjoy them. Use herbs like cilantro and culantro as a base to add flavor to your dishes. Recreate mami's delicious sancocho with veggies like yucca, batata, and auyama. Pack plenty of leafy greens and pico de gallo into your tacos. Next, add your preferred flavors to salads. You don't have to use the salad dressing options at your local supermarket. Instead, try something you actually crave, like a sprinkle of some chimichurri sauce or an avocado lime dip. One last tip: Include fruits as your snack and dessert choices to boost your plant intake even more.

Drink More Water

Amor, you're a brilliant, powerful, and bad mamisonga—and you're probably mad dehydrated.

Your body needs water. Agüita is your body's principal chemical component, making up about 50–70 percent of your body weight. Water removes waste from your cuerpo through perspiration, urination, and bowel movements. It keeps your body's temperature normal. It even protects your tissues and lubricates your joints. When you ignore your body's need for water, you end up dehydrated. Mild dehydration can cause headaches, dizzy spells, inability to focus, muscle weakness, and fatigue. More extreme forms of dehydration can result in heat injury, urinary and kidney problems, seizures, and low blood volume shock. Signs you're dehydrated include thirst, dry mouth, dark-colored urine, fatigue, dizziness, and confusion.

To prevent dehydration, drink plenty of water and eat water-rich foods like pineapples and papayas. The amount of water your body needs to stay healthy and hydrated is unique to you and your lifestyle. For instance, if you exercise or live in a warmer climate, you will need to drink more water throughout the day. To make sure you are always getting the agua your body needs, keep a reusable water bottle with you. When you have water nearby, you are more likely to drink when your body signals to you that it's thirsty. If your taste buds find water to be too boring, infuse it with mint, lime, or cucumbers. Remember: It's all about listening to what your cuerpo is communicating. So drink up.

Remember That
Bodies Change

Remember during puberty when your hips started to curve wider and, for some, your breasts began to develop? Whether these changes felt humiliating or long overdue, they were bound to happen. The body needs to transform as you enter the next stage in your aging life. And guess what: It never stops changing.

Whether you're in your twenties or your sixties, your body is ever evolving. You might be familiar with the cognitive and sensory changes that occur as you grow older, but your digestion also alters and you experience both muscle and bone loss. As a result, many women start to see an increase in body fat. These extra pounds could bump you up a size or two or may transform the shape of your body entirely. Or maybe you'll notice differences in your skin, from cellulite to wrinkles, or in the texture of your hair.

My love, this is as natural a process as it was when you first had to buy a bra. But in a society and culture that idealize the thin, young, and able-bodied, these changes might not be welcomed. So if you're feeling any uneasiness about these changes, know that you're understood. Try journaling about how you feel about your changing body or use a workbook like fat-liberation activist Virgie Tovar's *The Body Positive Journal* to help guide you. As you reflect, explore how your insecurities around being a glorious, aging, and ever-reshaping Latina woman stem from existing in a fatphobic, racist, ageist, and ableist culture, and recognize that *this* is the problem, not *you*.

Buy Clothes That Make You Feel Good in the Body You Have Right Now

Have you ever noticed that when you're dressed in your go-to mami chula 'fit, you feel as hot as you look? That's because how you dress has an effect on your psychology and your performance. According to a study by Northwestern University, through a process called enclothed cognition, many people ascribe meaning to clothing and this can impact how you think and feel when dressed in particular garbs.

Maybe you feel your best when you're stunting in red, whether that be your favorite scarlet lipstick shade, a cherry acrylic nail set, or a form-fitting wine-colored dress. Or perhaps you prefer the touch of certain fabrics on your skin, like a cotton loungewear set, a cashmere sweater, or a silk skirt. The styles that make you feel good are what you need in your closet, now. Not when you lose weight here or gain muscle there. Ahora. This body in this present moment deserves to be embellished in your favorite colors, patterns, textures, and fashions—and you deserve to feel fabulous in the clothes you wear.

When you have some free time, play your favorite playlist and sift through your closet, taking stock of what you own, what no longer fits, and what you love (or don't care for). If the garments you're discarding are in good condition, consider donating them to a loved one, a women's shelter, or a thrift shop. If you could use some extra coins, take them to a consignment store or sell them online instead.

Now that you have a better understanding of what you're into and what fits comfortably, start looking for pieces to add to your wardrobe. You con't have to break the bank. You can go to that same thrift store, consignment shop, or online secondhand marketplace. If you prefer to buy new, take it slow, treating yourself to an outfit once a month (or whatever you can afford). Play with what you already own and don't forget about hair, makeup, and accessories— if you're into that. Just make an effort to dress your beautiful and worthy body of today in 'fits that make you feel and look lovely.

Start a Facial Skincare Routine

Skin care is having a moment—but it's not just some throwaway fad. There are real wellness benefits to taking care of your skin. Your skin is your body's largest organ. All day, every day, it's protecting your body from bacteria, chemicals, and temperature changes. So keeping it clean, hydrated, and healthy is undoubtedly a form of body love and self-care. Even more, the act of engaging in a skincare regimen feels good. It's a pampering spa-like experience that also boosts your mood and eases stress.

If you're new to skin care, know that each person's routine is different because it's unique to their individual skin needs and cosmetic interests. Nonetheless, there are a few steps that are recommended by dermatologists for both daytime and nighttime skincare regimens.

- *The first step is cleansing your face. Whether you're waking up with drool on your chin, sweating from a morning workout, or removing your face paint after a long day, a gentle cleanser extracts the dirt, oils, makeup, sunscreen, and dead skin cells on your face and helps unclog your pores.*

- *Next, use a toner. A toner is a liquid-based formula that restores the skin's pH balance and helps smooth the skin by minimizing the appearance of pores.*

- *After that, apply products aimed at treating the skin. Skin conditions are extremely common, and many people incorporate products into their daily regimens aimed at healing or minimizing them. For instance, if you deal with acne, rosacea, or hyperpigmentation, to name a few, apply relevant products during this step. NOTE: Whether these creams or serums are purchased over the counter or prescribed by a dermatologist, know that these formulas tend to be harsher, so you may want to use them just once a day, a few times a week, or only when you're having a flare-up.*

- *Next, it's time to moisturize. Moisturizers replenish lost hydration in the skin and act as a barrier against various components.*

- *Finally, for morning routines, be sure to also use sunscreen to protect your skin throughout the day.*

Again, everyone's skin is different, even if they share a similar shade or texture, so you may need to try a few different formulas until you find one that works how you want it to. And there are amazing Latina-owned skincare brands, like Hyper Skin, SBJ Esntls, Sanara Skincare, and Brujita Skincare, that create products for people with various skin types, hues, and concerns.

Prioritize Solo Sex

Just about everywhere you look, Latinas are hypersexualized. According to a study by Pace University, Latinas are more likely to be oversexualized in film than women categorized in any other race or ethnicity. If you type "Latina" into Google or the search bar of most social media apps, the results will mostly include images of half-naked women and links to X-rated content. This portrayal of the always sexually available Latina is dangerous; it turns Latina bodies into objects to be consumed and discarded, regardless of our consent or pleasure. Solo sex is one way you can resist this gaze and explore your body, sexuality, and pleasure for yourself. Nadie más.

Solo sex is exactly what it sounds like: getting busy all by yourself. For sexual Latinas, this is hugely important. So often, Latinas are taught to be sexpots that perform for someone else's gratification. But when it comes to self-pleasure, it's all about you. Through masturbation, you are able to identify what it is that you like and don't like, and then touch yourself in all the ways that make you go "ooh" and "aah." Even more, you give yourself the chance to discover your fantasies, free from anyone else. Embracing your inner frikitona through solo sex is fun, empowering, and puts the attention where it belongs: on you.

In addition to this toe-curling placer, there are also numerous health benefits to solo sex. Physically, masturbation can ease pain, boost libido, and improve sleep. Mentally, it's known to relieve stress, make you feel happier and calmer, and even improve cognitive function. And if you're in a relationship, it can heighten sexual satisfaction and teach you what to ask for from your partner(s).

To prioritize solo sex, find ways to fit it into your schedule, even making it part of your morning or nighttime routine during certain days of the week. Next, romance yourself. Treat your senses by playing erotic music, dimming the lights and igniting a scented candle, dressing up in a little something that makes you feel sexy, and incorporating sex items like toys or pleasure oils from Latina-owned brands like Bloomi and Maude. Then, start slowly, gently rubbing the sensitive parts of your body, like your thighs and breasts. Enjoy the foreplay for as long as you'd like, and when you're ready, stimulate your highly erogenous zones. For women with vulvas, direct clitoral stimulation is often, though not always, the most satisfying. For women with penises, the head has the highest concentration of nerve endings. Make it last for as short or as long as you'd like. This is all about you, so switch positions if you want to, introduce other forms of erotica, and look at yourself in the mirror—if you want to.

Ask for What You Want in Bed During Partnered Sex

Whether you're in a long-term relationship or seeing someone casually, it can be intimidating to ask for what you want in bed. But, mami, your sexual pleasure is part of your radical self-care, so if your needs aren't being met, you have to communicate that.

As media images have produced a patriarchal fantasy of Latinas as sexually available for all, a culture of marianismo has taught you to be chaste and subservient in relationships. During partnered sex, these mixed messages may have tempted you to perform a racial-ized sexuality in bed that gives more than it receives. And it may have left you uncomfortable about having your own sexual desires. If your sexual curiosities frighten you, you are less likely to spend time thinking about them, which makes knowing what to ask for during sex complicated. And even if you do have an idea of what you like or don't like, these internalized beliefs around sex may make you anxious about voicing those yearnings.

But no matter what has stopped you from voicing what you want with a sexual partner in the past, you can move beyond this and learn how to communicate your sexual preferences. To start, have an open mind. Your sexual wellness will include unlearning the shame you were taught. Next, be clear about what you want. If you're unsure, think about it some more and perhaps introduce these desires into your solo sessions.

After this, determine if your requests would be better asked during sex or outside of it. For instance, quick adjustments, like ask-ing your partner(s) to go faster or slower or move a little more to the left or right, are great to voice while you're in action. But if you want to introduce new experiences, like bringing in a third, testing out a sex toy, or trying a different position, you should set aside some time to talk. Try practicing the discussion beforehand. Then schedule the conversation with your partner, letting them know that you'd like to talk about your sex life so the conversation doesn't surprise them. During the sex discussion, use "I" statements so that you are taking ownership of what you want from the sexual relationship. Avoid attacking them or comparing them to past partners. You don't want to hurt anyone's feelings; that's not what this is about. Instead, let them know that this is something you want to explore with them, and encourage them to open up to you as well.

Practice Safe Sex

Beba, are you having sex safely? Every time? According to the National Institutes of Health, Latinas are less likely to use contraception than other women. And Latina immigrants, in particular, have a higher risk of using ineffective contraception or using effective contraception inconsistently.

The reasons Latinas are getting intimate without protections against STIs and unplanned pregnancies are numerous: Latinas are more likely to grow up in homes where sex and sexuality aren't discussed. Latinas often live in states that teach abstinence-only sex education, a curriculum that doesn't arm students with the resources needed to enjoy their sexual bodies safely. Latinas, and especially immigrant Latinas, are less likely to have health insurance and may have difficulty paying for birth control, in particular, consistently. And Latinas are more likely to experience intimate-partner violence in relationships that may impact the use of contraception.

But by not practicing safer sex every time, you put yourself at greater risk of contracting infections and diseases as well as having an unwanted pregnancy. In fact, Latinas are disproportionately affected by HIV and other STIs, like chlamydia and gonorrhea, than non-Latine white women. Also, Latinas are more likely to have an unplanned pregnancy.

To practice safer sex, talk with your partner(s) openly about sexual health. Ask them when they were last tested and what their results were. Regardless of their response, use a barrier method, like a condom or diaphragm, during sex, including sex that doesn't involve penis-to-vagina penetration. If you're using a sex toy with a partner, still use a condom. If you are using a lubricant, make sure it's compatible with your condom. For instance, oil-based lubes can damage latex condoms and break them. Water-based or silicone lubes are generally safe to use with any kind of barrier method. If you are someone who is capable of conceiving a pregnancy, consider going on hormonal birth control. There are multiple options, including the pill, vaginal ring, patches, and more. Finally, get tested for STIs every three to six months. Remember: You deserve to enjoy your sexual body without unwanted outcomes, and any partner who doesn't agree with that doesn't deserve *you*.

Take a Warm Bath

Mami, have you experienced the restorative powers of a bañera? If not, you're missing out. Soaking in a bath is an ancient wellness practice that can relieve muscle aches and pain and heal certain skin conditions. Immersing yourself en agua may even ease anxiety, help you unwind, and prepare you for quality sleep.

Start by turning your bath into a multisensory-stimulating experience. Turn the lights off and ignite a candle, or several, instead. Play some soothing music, like ambient sounds that transport you to a Central American waterfall or some old-school boleros. Elevate the restorative powers of the water by sprinkling in some Epsom salt, bath bombs, bubbles, or flower petals. Latine-owned brands like Loquita Bath, Terra, Nopalera, Maude, and Becalia Botanicals sell bath essentials inspired by Latin American and Caribbean wellness practices. Turn on the water, bringing it to a warm temperature that is relaxing and safe for your skin. Once the tub is filled halfway with water, tiptoe in. For about ten to twenty minutes, maximum, allow yourself to soak. You can rest in the water or entertain your inner child by playing with bubbles. You can take the time to enjoy doing nothing, or you can do some light reading.

Once you're out of the tub, dry, and lolling under a sabana, you won't underestimate the transformative abilities of a bath again. As so many Latina elders say, respeta las aguas.

Enjoy a Warm Tea

There's a reason the señoras in your life brewed up some tea when you fell ill as a child. These warm beverages are made with plantitas and hierbas that have healing properties that have nursed people to wellness for centuries. And the health advantages of a soothing té are always available to you.

According to a study by the National Institutes of Health, drinking tea is a health-promoting habit. For instance, the *Camellia sinensis* plant, a shrub found in green and black teas, contains antioxidants that help prevent some cancers, cardiovascular diseases, and clogged arteries. There is evidence that some properties in teas help alleviate stress and reduce risk of neurological disorders like Alzheimer's and Parkinson's diseases. Knowing that Latinas are more likely to have certain risk factors for heart disease and to develop Alzheimer's than the general population, it's important that this practice of sipping home-brewed tea throughout the day, like some of your elders may have done back in your country of origin, is preserved.

To consume more té, first discover what you like. Teas often have an earthy taste that may take some time to get used to if you didn't grow up drinking them. Ask the elders in your family how they make their tea or research some infusions that are common in your matria. For instance, mate teas, prepared with the dried ground leaves of the yerba mate plant, are popular in South America, while it's more common to infuse hibiscus in Caribbean teas. Next, turn teatime into a ritual. Savor it during breaks or add it to the wellness practices you're already enjoying, like sipping on tea during a bath, while you have a face mask on, or ahead of a massage. However you fit it in, just drink up, preciosa.

Go on a Hike

Imagine you're outside on a trail. As you walk along the path, the sun warms your back and the wind provides a welcome relief. The crackling leaves beneath your feet join the chorus of birds chirping, insects humming, and water splashing. You're one with nature, just how your ancestors lived once upon a time. That closeness to land—even if it's far away from the place they once traversed—feels like home. This is the enchantment of hiking.

For many, hiking is medicine, and its properties heal the body, mind, and spirit. That's because hiking is a multilayered exercise. Physically, it improves heart health; supports your respiratory system; strengthens your muscles, joints, and bones; and improves your balance. Mentally, strolling through nature reduces stress and calms anxiety. Spiritually, spending time outdoors helps you take stock of all the aspects of your life that you are grateful for and connects you to all living beings.

And amor, you don't have to be a survivalist or an outdoorsy kind of gal to trudge the land. Start by choosing a beginner-friendly trail. This might look like a short, cleared path, one with little-to-no hills, or perhaps one with rest areas along the way. Once you've selected your location, research what kinds of animals, insects, and plants you'll find there, and how to react if you encounter them; it's good to know what to expect in terms of flora and fauna. Next, pack what you'll need. Just because you've seen hikers sporting heavy backpacks and walking with poles doesn't mean you need them too. Start out with comfortable sneakers or boots, a reusable water bottle, sunscreen, bug repellent, a hat, and a bag of trail mix in case you need an energy boost. Also, be sure to dress for the weather.

Finally, decide if you want to hike alone or with a friend or join a group of hiking enthusiasts. If you are hitting the trails solo, tell someone you trust about your plans, including where, when, and for how long you expect to be trekking. To avoid getting lost or hurt, don't venture off the trail and avoid putting on headphones. You need to stay alert and aware of your surroundings. If you prefer to join a group, there are collectives like Latinxhikers, Hike Clerb, Vida Verde, and Latino Outdoors that organize hikes by and for Latines and other communities of color.

Moisturize Your Skin

Your skin is a complex organ that protects you from pathogens all day, every day. But to work effectively, your skin needs to be properly hydrated. We discussed taking care of the skin on your face in the Start a Facial Skincare Routine entry, and now we'll focus on the rest of your body. When your skin is dry, you're vulnerable to various skin conditions. Lathering your piel with hydrating ointments like body butters and lotions strengthens this organ, makes you smooth to the touch, and nourishes your body.

However, any ol' lotion on your pharmacy store shelf might not be sufficient for you. A report published in the *Journal of Clinical and Aesthetic Dermatology* found that it's not just external factors, like climate, temperature, and washing, that impact the dryness of your skin; your race does as well. Despite the racial variability of skin, most moisturizers on the market are made for less-pigmented skin, making these formulas potentially less effective on melanated mamis. So while all Latinas need to be moisturizing, Black Latinas and brown Latinas, especially those of you who have roots in arid climates, need to find formulas that work for your skin. Brands like the Afro-Latina-owned SunKiss Organics carry full-body skincare products for women with darker skin.

After you've found a body butter or lotion that your skin loves, you need to make sure you're applying and reapplying it. During a shower or bath, your piel gets very dry, so you need to moisturize immediately afterward. Rub some extra balm on your driest areas, which tend to be your hands, elbows, knees, and feet. When you're all lotioned up, you'll physically feel better, and not *just* because you're velvety smooth. You adorned your whole body with tender love and care, and that sweet sensation you're experiencing is your skin whispering gracias.

Take the Plunge

Cold plunging is all the rage right now, with non-Latines traveling to Chile and Argentina to dive into glacial waters to remedy aches and pains, decrease inflammation, reduce swelling, promote lymphatic drainage, or simply enjoy the rush of endorphins and dopamine that comes from freezing temperatures. But as Cindy Luquin argues in an essay for *Refinery29 Somos*, it's also a spiritual practice. The therapy of soaking in frigid water has been a way of life for people throughout Latin America and the Caribbean for a long time, with some Afro-Caribbean and Indigenous spiritualities encouraging cold baths to heal the body and rid the spirit of negative energy.

Instead of traveling long distances and preparing your body for arctic-cold water immersion, you can experience the wellness qualities of cold therapy at spas, swimming pools, or even your own bathroom. If you have a bathtub, fill it up halfway with cold water. Next, add about three to five pounds of ice to cool the water even more. Slowly, descend into the bath until you are fully immersed, taking deep breaths along the way to lower your heart rate.

Don't stay in the icy water for too long. Too much exposure can lead to shock or hypothermia, so start with just a couple minutes before working yourself up to eight or ten minutes, maximum.

As an alternative to the tub, hop in the shower when the water is at its coldest. Sure, it might not be as chilly as an ice bath, but it will still get your blood flowing and help alleviate some pains.

If soaking your body in frigid showers and baths feels like too much, you can simply dip your toes in the cold plunge waters for a therapeutic foot bath.

Get Your Nails Done

While self-care is much more than manis and pedis, getting your nails done can radically improve how you feel. Latinas have a long relationship with nail care and design. For years, you may have accompanied your mami to the local nail salon (or, let's be real, some señora's house) and sat for an hour-plus getting your finger-nails cleaned, cut, and embellished with an elaborate design. When you two left, you didn't just feel rejuvenated by the water-jet foot spa and the lotioned hand massage. Y'all also felt like the mamison-gas of the block, straight stuntin' with your gel or acrylic set. That's the power of your mani-pedi appointment: It's both relaxing and confidence boosting.

To treat yourself, make an appointment with your favorite nail technician. If you don't have one, look for nail artists in your area. You can go to one of the many neighborhood nail salons or book with a licensed, self-employed Latina nail tech. Next, consider the type of manicure and pedicure you want, the nail design and color you're interested in, and if you want to use a nontoxic nail polish, gel, acrylic, or gel-X. If you prefer vegan or nontoxic lacquer, like Latina-owned brands Lights Lacquer and Passport Polish, don't be shy to bring your own. Finally, when it's appointment day, put your phone aside and be fully present in the moment. Enjoy being pam-pered, refreshed, and glamorized. You deserve to unwind and feel like the baddie that you are.

Go to the Hair Salon

Going to the hair salon can be physically, mentally, and spiritually rejuvenating. For Latinas, it's a sanctuary, a safe space where you enter to unload, in all the ways. You let your hair down, confident that your hairdresser will cut, color, and/or style your tresses back to health and beauty. But you also let your guard down, trusting that the chisme about life and work that you need to externalize will be validated and held safe by the stylists and patrons who can all relate. On top of it all, you're resting on a salon chair while someone twirls you around as they massage your scalp and brush your hair. It's therapeutic, mama, and it's time to book your next appointment.

For a trip to the hair salon to feel truly sanative, you have to go somewhere you feel safe. If your hairdresser repeatedly tells you that you have "pelo malo," judges your tales or identity, or never really gives you what you asked for, that spot ain't it. It doesn't matter if you've been seeing that stylist for most of your life or if your home-girls frequent the same salon. It's time to move on. You deserve to feel heard while you're sitting on that salon chair and love what you see when you get up and look in the mirror, especially when you're paying for these services. You might need to test out a few stylists and salons to find your safe haven.

To get the most out of your salon experience, book hair appointments in advance and prepare to be there for a while. You already know how it is. If you plan to be in and out, you're only setting yourself up for frustration and unease. Instead, carve out a few hours for this time and indulge in all the pampering and joy you deserve.

Start a Haircare Routine

Hair love shouldn't start or end at the hair salon. To keep your hair and scalp healthy, create a home haircare ritual that works for you. Like skin, hair varies in color, type, texture, and conditions. And Latinas, who come in every race and ethnic makeup conceivable, have different hair needs and concerns. Maybe you struggle with a flaky scalp or root frizz. Perhaps your natural coils are breaking or your straight hair is thinning. Regardless, your haircare routine should be as unique as you.

The first step is identifying your natural hair type and texture. Hair can be straight, wavy, curly, or Afro-textured. The strands can be thin or thick. And the natural color can range from brown, to blonde, to red. Next, figure out what conditions you are hoping to alleviate, like restoring chemically processed strands or calming an itchy scalp. Finally, research products especially made for your hair type and concerns and incorporate those into your routine. Ask your hair stylist for recommendations or shop at stores that offer sample sizes if you don't want to spend too much money testing out different products.

For a basic regimen, begin with a shampoo and conditioner. If you feel like you need more from these products, test a clarifying shampoo or a leave-in or deep conditioner. Next, moisturize with oils or hair lotions. To avoid breakage, use a detangling spray or serum when brushing or combing your hair. For routines that target your individual hair needs, you might also want to use over-the-counter or prescribed treatments and/or protective products like silk and satin hair caps and pillow cases. Latina-owned brands like

Bomba Curls, Ceremonia, Rizos Curls, and Hello Updo sell products and treatments for all hair types and concerns.

Finally, as you work with your hair, be kind to yourself. Due to colonialism, you may have deeply internalized Eurocentric beauty ideals. Depending on your race, you may have accepted the white supremacist myth of pelo bueno and pelo malo, which extols thin, straight tresses that are more common among white Latinas while denigrating thick, Afro-textured coils that are natural to many Black Latinas. Or, if you are Indigenous, you may have been teased for having dark, long, thick, and straight hair. To decolonize these beauty standards and celebrate your natural hair, consider styling your mane how your ancestors may have, from Afros and cornrows to las trenzas de las Adelitas and braid crowns.

Taking the time to regularly clean, treat, protect, and style your hair won't just revitalize your hair; it'll also rejuvenate you wholly, leaving you feeling refreshed and taken care of.

Wear Sunscreen

Do you wear sunscreen every day? If not, you need to start incorporating SPF into your daily skincare regimen. While Latinas are less likely to develop skin cancers, like melanoma, than non-Latine white women, Latinas are more likely to die from these diseases. The reason: Latinas tend to get diagnosed with skin cancers later because, in addition to skimping on sunblock, Latinas are also not taking regular trips to the dermatologist's office. Even more, a study published in the *Journal of Drugs in Dermatology* in 2019 found that melanoma has risen by 20 percent among Latines.

Amor, you have to wear sunscreen. Every day. Everywhere. It doesn't matter how melanated your skin is; you have to protect it from the sun's dangerous rays. To start, find a sunblock that you like, preferably one that's long-lasting, sweat-resistant, and doesn't leave your skin all ghostly. Be sure to use an SPF of at least 30. This blocks about 97 percent of the sun's ultraviolet B (UVB) rays.

Make sunblock part of your daily facial skincare routine, adding it to the very end of your regimen before putting on any makeup. If you'll be out in the sun for a while, keep sunscreen with you to reapply throughout the day, ideally every two hours. And, baby girl, please make it a habit to go to the dermatologist for regular skin checks, especially if new moles arise. Your glorious piel deserves to be protected.

Try a New Latin American or Caribbean Restaurant Once a Month

Self-care includes treating yourself. And sometimes the best gift you can give yourself is getting out of the cocina and letting someone else cook for you. And if you are going to be wined and dined, make sure it's that good-good. Food should be relished. To savor the flavors you crave without putting in kitchen work, dine at your local Latin American or Caribbean restaurant.

Eating meals you grew up with doesn't just nourish your body; it also feeds your mind and spirit. When you smell the onions, garlic, peppers, and herbs of sofrito in the kitchen of a Puerto Rican restaurant or hear the sizzling of a smoky, zesty fajita at a Mexican eatery, your body releases dopamine that makes you feel as delicious as the meal you're about to ingest.

To delight your taste buds, make it a tradition to try a new Latin American or Caribbean restaurant once a month. First, decide what kind of food you want to enjoy. You can patronize cuchifritos that feel like home or try the scrumptious and distinct flavors of different países and regions. Peru is a world-leading culinary destination, so if you have a Peruvian restaurant by you, add it to your list, ASAP. Meanwhile, Salvadoran pupusas are guaranteed to hit, every single time. Next, make this a moment to share space with loved ones, especially if they come from a different cultural background. Let them put you on to their faves and marvel at the way your ancestors created different plates with similar ingredients.

When you're all done, tip well. You'll be supporting workers at Latine-owned businesses—and spoiling yourself in the most succulent of ways.

Rebuild Your Relationship with Cultural Foods

Latinas have disproportionately high rates of eating disorders and disordered eating. For Latinas, the risk factors for developing an ED mirror that of other communities—trauma, abuse, early puberty, culture—but are often compounded by racial and xenophobic violence. Similarly, Latinas also face an increased risk due to acculturation, the expectation that you must literally slim the parts of yourself that the dominant culture claims aren't acceptable. Oftentimes, this includes your body and the foods you eat.

From grade-school health classes to the enormous (and fatphobic) diet industry, you have been taught that your cuisine is bad. Diet culture has fed you the myth that the nourishing Garifuna hudut or Brazilian feijoada you grew up eating has no health benefits. It sells you the lie that the ingredients that sustained your ancestors for generations, and through colonization, violence, and natural calamities, are harmful. It's time to call bullshit.

In truth, it's narratives of restriction and denial that are damaging Latinas by inducing self-hate, fear of cultural foods, and disordered eating. You can push back by reclaiming the flavors of your traditional fare and incorporating them through education. Because, yes, it is wise to sprinkle more plants onto your dishes. But guess what? Latin America and the Caribbean have an abundance of root vegetables that you can add to—and are likely already on—your plate. If you need some help—and there's nothing wrong with it if you do—consider working with a Latina dietitian or nutritionist. Accredited experts like Dalina Soto of Your Latina Nutritionist can help you create a healthful diet that considers your individual nutritional needs, past relationship with food, and present lifestyle.

Floss Your Teeth

How often do you floss your teeth? Be honest, sis. Most people don't floss every day, and about a quarter of folks lie about how often they floss. But you don't have to fib, baby girl, because you're not going to judge yourself regardless of what your answer is. Instead, you're just going to make it a habit to clean between your pretty little teeth.

Flossing regularly is necessary to maintain dental hygiene. When you skip this step before brushing your teeth, plaque begins to build up, causing your grill to decay and stink. But flossing your teeth keeps your pearly dientes polished and fresh smelling while also reducing the risk of cavities and gum disease. This is vital, period, but especially for you, mama. According to a report from the Centers for Disease Control and Prevention (CDC), Latines are less likely to see a dentist regularly than non-Latine white folks. And if you're skipping on those annual cleanings and exams, then you should be doing everything else you can to keep your teeth healthy.

To start, find a floss that you prefer. There are floss threads that are waxed or unwaxed, flavored or unflavored, braces-friendly, and biodegradable. There are flossers and dental picks. And there are water flossers. Once you've picked your preference, keep the floss visible in your bathroom so that you don't forget to use it at least once a day. Finally, you should floss before you brush so that your toothpaste can reach between your plaque-reduced teeth.

Work Standing Up

If you're able to, stand up. Like right now. Just by getting on your feet you are tending to your body. When you stand upright, you improve your posture and reduce back pain. Even more, you get your heart beating, improving your cardiovascular health, and your blood sugar levels drop. Standing, as opposed to sitting or lying down, also boosts your energy, focus, and mood. Not so bad for movement that most people can do pretty easily, huh?

Despite the considerable health benefits of standing, about one-third of people in the US are sedentary. More and more, jobs require employees to sit at their desks all day. And this can seriously harm your health. For instance, people who are stationary throughout the day are at greater risk of developing diabetes and heart disease, two illnesses Latinas may be at high risk for.

If you're able-bodied, try to stand more throughout your day. One of the easiest ways to fit this in your day is by carrying out work tasks while on your feet. There are standing desks and adjustable desks that allow you to change the height of the table so that you can alternate between sitting and standing throughout the day.

If these desks are not available at your workplace, ask your boss if the company can pay for a desk upgrade; after all, it'll benefit your health and, subsequently, your attendance and productivity on the job. If you work for yourself and an adjustable desk is out of your price range, there are more cost-effective adaptable laptop stands that you can place on your desk and move to sitting and standing heights.

However, if you'd rather, or need to, sit while you work, that's fine too. You can still benefit from getting up on your feet. Schedule in a few minutes every hour to stand, stretch, and go for a short walk. Or you can initiate walk-and-talk meetings with coworkers or use a headset so that you can stand while taking phone calls. For optimal health, it's generally recommended to stand for at least two hours a day, but you can start with fifteen minutes here and thirty minutes there and still reap all the rewards.

Advocate for Your Health

Latinas have a tangled history with the US medical system. For some, immigration status, a lack of health insurance, and/or poverty makes preventive care and treatment inaccessible. For others, there's a distrust in healthcare rooted in a history of medical experiments on Latina bodies, as well as a legacy of mistreatment and misdiagnosis that discourages Latinas from seeking medical attention altogether.

But not seeing a physician regularly or scheduling medical tests when concerns arise is killing Latinas. In fact, Latinas are more likely to be diagnosed with fatal illnesses like cancers when these diseases are at later stages, worsening the chances for effective treatment.

As a Latina, you may need to put in more time, effort, and energy to ensure healthcare providers are listening to you and taking your concerns seriously. Speaking up can feel distressing, intimidating, and even like an unfair burden, but you *must* advocate for yourself—your life depends on it.

To start, educate yourself. Know when and how often you are supposed to get regular screenings, recognizing that your own family history might require you to get tested earlier or more often than someone else. Schedule these appointments, *now*. Don't tell yourself it's too far in advance or make an excuse for why it can wait. The sooner you get these appointments in your calendar, the more likely you are to find dates and times that fit your schedule. Next, listen to your body. Practicing regular body scans will help you identify when your body is in fine health and when something is off. If you start experiencing pain or notice a change in your body, like a lump or a mole, don't ignore it and don't put it off. Schedule an appointment with your doctor immediately. Finally, write out your symptoms and your concerns. Similarly, make a list of your and your family's health history.

Take all of this information with you to your appointment so that you can communicate it to your doctor. If you need support, bring a trusted friend or relative along with you. If you feel like your symptoms are being dismissed or ignored by your primary physician, ask for a referral to a specialist or go to a different practice for a second opinion. And when you're done, find yourself a new primary care provider, someone who makes you feel heard and comfortable.

Reclaim Your Bodily Autonomy

As a Latina, there may have been times in your life when you felt like your body was not yours. Throughout history, Latina bodies have been used as subjects for medical tests, like sterilization and birth control pill experimentation. Often these tests were performed without informed consent.

Additionally, for generations, popular media has fetishized the Latina body. Latinas are portrayed as objects to be sexualized, consumed, and discarded by men. More recently, non-Latine white women have capitalized on the curvaceous Latina stereotype by promoting and undergoing procedures like Brazilian butt lifts (BBLs).

However, as the beauty benchmark shifts back to thinner shapes, many of these same women have undergone BBL reductions, once again rejecting a body type that is natural and common for many, though certainly not all, Black and brown women. Over and over, the Latina body is chewed up and thrown out, rarely with apology, and frequently without consent.

When you feel like you don't have control over your body, you start to become disconnected from it. If you have experienced physical or sexual trauma, you might even begin to disassociate from your body.

But it's time to reclaim your bodily autonomy. To start, you first have to process the trauma or experiences that prompted this unlinking. You can begin to do this through therapy, journaling, and other mental health self-care practices.

Then, assign culpability where it belongs, whether it be to a person, system, or culture, and free yourself from any guilt or shame for existing in your body.

Next, reconnect with your body. You can do this by engaging in physical practices, like dance, sports, or other body movement, that help you become more embodied and present with your physical self.

This process may take some time, but this, amor, is how you begin to reclaim ownership of your body.

part three

Spirit

Your spirit might be intangible, but caring for it is integral to your overall wellness. Your soul is your inner being; it's the essence of who you are. When your spirit is unwell, you feel it. Even other souls can sense when you're dispirited. It's invisible but somehow still discernible. It sucks the energy out of a room; it lowers the vibration. Conversely, when your spirit is flourishing, when your vibrations are high, it's arousing. It dazzles other souls and nourishes your own mental and physical health.

Your soul is healthy when you are in line with your true self; when you treat yourself with unconditional love, respect, and kindness; and when it feels deeply connected to other spirits. In this section, you'll find exercises that reinvigorate your soul. These actions will help you come home to your soul self by reconnecting you with your innermost being, your higher power, your ancestors, your living and deceased community, and the land you occupy. You will learn about ancient spiritual traditions practiced by people across Latin America and the Caribbean for centuries, and you will be given new actions designed specifically for Latinas like you. You don't have to be religious to be spiritual, and you can follow one faith and incorporate other spiritual practices into your self-care regimen. You deserve to operate as your highest self.

Embark on Your Señora Era

Remember visiting la casita de abuelita in the homeland and seeing how she lived so presently in every moment? Whether it's a memory from a time before you migrated or during a childhood trip, try to return there for a moment. Picture her: savoring her morning cafecito, swaying to boleros by Olga Guillot and Toña la Negra while still dressed in her bata, and fanning herself as she looks out the window, taking in nature's vista.

Abuelita was, and continues to be, goals. And you can follow her lead. At a time when so many Latinas feel overworked, overscheduled, and overstimulated, deciding to live life more presently allows you to push back against hustle culture and avoid burnout. The reason abuelita knew to live in the moment was that she had the wisdom of her years. Life had already taught her how quickly time moves and how fleeting moments are. By being in your señora era, you can embrace her wisdom sooner rather than later—you can protect your time and create moments for rest, curiosity, and simple pleasures.

To embark on your señora journey, appreciate what you have right now and live your life knowing that tomorrow may not come. Do something you love today, not when you're in a relationship or when your kids are older. Do something that enlivens you now, not when you get that promotion or retire. Ahora. You don't have to abandon your responsibilities and live life cloistered on a farm. That's not realistic for everyone. But take a look at your calendar and your planner. Recognize how you're spending your time, and ask yourself if it's really worthwhile. Are you busy because you need to be or because you are afraid not to be? You can replace unnecessary obligations with something you genuinely love. Permission granted. You can simply be—unrushed, en el momento, y con tu bata puesta.

Clean Your Space While Dancing to Your Favorite Songs

Remember when you were a kid and mami used to wake up early on the weekends blasting a mix of salsa, merengue, and freestyle classics as she cleaned the crib? She used la escoba as her microphone, serving face and lip quivers while she gave her best interpretation of Milly Quezada. And she strutted through the house like Rosie Perez on the *Soul Train* line, bumping, grinding, and spinning herself to a squeaky-clean home. Mami understood the power of habit stacking long before TikTok made it a trend, turning something she had to do, limpiar la casa, into a whole pari. She was onto something.

According to a study published in the journal *Personality and Social Psychology Bulletin*, cleaning your space instills you with a sense of control, boosts your mood, and can make you feel calm. In other words, a casita that feels polished and in order can revitalize your spirit. Add some good tunes, especially old-school jams that transport you to breezy memories of a time when your workload and worries were less heavy, and your soul will feel so uplifted, even if you have sweat dripping from your forehead.

To start, make a nostalgic playlist. You might want to include 1980s baladas, 1990s reggae en español and reggaetón, 2000s bachata, and even some of those spiritually elevating coritos if you grew up en la iglesia. When your mix is ready, blast it from your phone, TV, or home speakers and get ready to scrub and organize. Whether it's a seasonal deep-clean or a Sunday reset, allow your soul to be swept up by the music, and sing and dance your way into a sanctuary.

Take a Trip to Your Ancestral Land

There is something spiritually nourishing about returning to the land of your ancestors. In many ways, traversing their grounds and detecting their likeness in the faces, accents, and mannerisms of so many other people makes you feel closer to yourself. These trips might introduce you to relatives you never met, or even knew existed. They could reveal stories, both painful and inspiring, about your family lineage. They may reconnect you to foods, music, art, spiritualities, and ways of life that were taken from you. Each of these experiences feeds your soul, helping you grow and, possibly, heal.

To be clear, your ancestral land can be anywhere that your predecessors lived, including continents deep in your genealogical history and the many countries or cities your forebears migrated to, some by force, others by reluctant choice. These trips could take you to countries or territories across Latin America and the Caribbean or may transport you to Africa, Europe, or Asia. But they can also send you to Texas's Rio Grande Valley; New York City's Washington Heights; Miami's Little Havana; Chicago's Humboldt Park; Washington, DC's Mount Pleasant; or Los Angeles's Boyle Heights—areas your family may have first migrated to many generations ago.

To start planning your ancestral trip, establish what your goals are for this journey. If you hope to explore and reconnect with your heritage, perhaps your itinerary might include frequenting special sites, enjoying the arts, and touring local farms and eateries to learn more about the cuisine. If you prefer a genealogy visit, you will need to spend more time, and perhaps money, researching your family's life in their homeland so that you can visit your abuelita's childhood home or locate a distant relative. From there, you can start saving money for the travel, lodging, experiences, and, if needed, genealogists to curate and guide your personalized trip.

It must be noted that being able to take an ancestral trip is, in many ways, a privilege that isn't available to every Latina due to immigration status, money, disabilities, or difficulty tracing one's history. In these cases, an ancestral voyage can take place through reading books or virtually experiencing someone else's travels.

While these visits are often complicated, going back to your family's place of origin teaches you complex histories that may help you make better sense of your relatives and the decisions they had to make. This deeper understanding of your cultural identity and migrational history can make you feel like you belong, inducing feelings of self-confidence, self-love, pride, and purpose that reinvigorate your soul.

Visit La Playita

Close your eyes and imagine yourself somewhere serene. Did it include water? For many people, blue space—beaches, rivers, springs, lakes, creeks, and other bodies of water—elicits feelings of both relaxation and joy. And it makes sense. Exposure to agüita has been linked to improving overall well-being, like lowering stress, elevating mood, and promoting a sense of balance. It's why so many travelers vacation at beach towns and others pay steep mortgages to live by the water.

But for Latinas, bathing en aguas naturales is also a deeply spiritual experience. In Aztec mythology, Chalchiuhtlicue is the water goddess, a mighty deity that protects and sustains life. For the ancient Maya people, water, especially cenotes, are gateways to other worlds that are inhabited by supernatural beings and spirits of those who passed away. In Afro-Cuban spiritual practices like Santería, ritual cleansings, or limpiezas that incorporate water and herbs or other items help maintain spiritual and physical well-being.

But whether you soak your body in beach water or not, the sound of waves crashing, ocean breezes fanning your skin, and powdery sand blanketing your toes are luxuries for your mind, body, and soul. And it's time for you to revel in Mama Tierra's wholesome gifts.

First, decide what kind of beach trip you're interested in having. Do you want to spend a week at a tropical beach in the Dominican Republic, or do you just need to end the day by driving to a local playa to catch the sunset from the seashore? Next, decipher what type of beach excursion your soul is asking you for. Maybe you need to unwind with a book and some fresh coconut water. Or perhaps what you need is to turn up in the salt water with your corillo as Bad

Bunny's baritone booms from a portable speaker. Both can be spiritually revitalizing.

If you are landlocked, and taking a quick dip into the sea, a spring, or a river isn't so easy for you, consider planning your next vacation at a destination known for its blue space. If a road trip or flight away isn't presently realistic for you, soak your body in a pool, Jacuzzi, or bathtub while playing soft ocean sounds. This at-home, spa-like experience can also be restorative.

Create a Playlist with Natural Sounds That Remind You of Home

From water rushing over rocks to critters jumping along branches, nature's symphony is a natural remedy that aids the spirit and the mind. A study published in the *Proceedings of the National Academy of Sciences* found that outdoor sounds minimize stress and pain and actually elevate feelings of joy, confidence, and community. Whether you're physically outside, basking in Mama Tierra's splendor, or indoors listening to a recording of earth's music, the sounds inspire you to let your guard down, where you are free to relax, create, or simply be.

While you might experience the wellness benefits of nature's songs regardless of the environment producing the score, to really enliven your soul, tune into the melodies of nature in your homeland. Listen to the roaring cascade of Venezuela's Angel Falls, the slurred notes of Guatemala's resplendent quetzal bird, the giggle of Peruvian llamas, or the whistling of Puerto Rico's coquíes. Latin America and the Caribbean are home to a vast number of natural world wonders as well as flora and fauna that all sing their own gorgeous arias. Many of these sounds have been captured and shared on streaming or social media platforms, like YouTube, where you can tune into your tierra's lullabies. This is how you gently cradle your soul.

Help Teach English to a New Migrant

Wars, political upheaval, natural disasters, and deep poverty have forced people all over the world, and especially across Latin America and the Caribbean, to emigrate from their homelands to remote countries where locals speak foreign tongues. As a Latina, you may intimately know, or have heard oral histories from relatives, about how your own family was uprooted from your land of origin and migrated to the country you currently call home. While each person's migration story is nuanced, it's a shared experience that connects you with so many other Latinas, immigrants, and children of immigrants. And it's this understanding that may encourage and prepare you to teach English to new migrants.

Whether you're certified to teach English as a foreign language through community programs, online classes, or English for Speakers of Other Languages (ESOL) education, or you're simply fluent in English and another language and want to support someone as they navigate an entirely different culture, doing so can make a sizable difference in their life—and yours as well. Multiple studies have found that giving back is good for your overall well-being, making you happier, filling you with a sense of purpose, and helping you feel connected. These are all ingredients that fortify your spirit.

Even more, whether you are teaching your abuelito English verb conjugation, working with someone through a mobile app like HelloTalk, or spending an hour every week on the phone helping that señora from your job or church feel more comfortable speaking English, you are making your ancestors and community so proud.

Acknowledge the Land You Occupy

History books write about colonization as if it's some blight from the past, but colonialism is an ongoing process. Not only are territories like Puerto Rico modern-day colonies of the US, but this nation continues to occupy stolen Indigenous land with little acknowledgment of how its history of genocide and displacement continues to harm Indigenous populations today. And, mami, if you inhabit this land now, too, and don't have an ancestral connection to it, then it's also incumbent on you to acknowledge to whom the land where you currently reside belongs.

Understanding this local history, including the complicated treaties that remain in effect, the correct pronunciation of names of tribes and places, the living Indigenous people from these communities, and the ways you can support them, is a start in minimizing violence. You can also donate your time and money to support local Indigenous organizations and campaigns as well as commit to land-returning projects.

Acknowledging the land you occupy is both a responsibility and a spiritual practice. When you know the history of the land and tribes who originally populated it, you are more inclined to care for your local environment, live in gratitude, and intentionally honor and celebrate Indigenous communities. And for some Latinas, especially those who have long lived in the Southwest, you might discover that you can trace your own lineage to local Indigenous tribes.

Build an Altar

As night falls on Día de Muertos, the homes of many Mexicans and Mexican Americans glow orange, with the fire of flickering candles making visible bright marigolds and photos of loved ones who have passed on. During the Mexican holiday, celebrated on November 1 and 2, families gather to honor the lives of the deceased and create ofrendas, home altars, with the departed's favorite foods, drinks, and other items in case they visit from the afterlife. It's a spiritual tradition that deepens bonds with loved ones, living and dead.

But across Latin America and the Caribbean, the practice of building and maintaining altars occurs year-round. Latinas, Latin Americans, and caribeñas of all religions and spiritualities use altars to connect them to the spirit life, including higher powers, ancestors, and guides.

To build an altar, first set your intention. Why do you want to create it? How do you want to elevate your spiritual life and/or who do you want to honor? Next, find a location that feels right for you. Some people want their altar to be private, so they keep it in their bedroom. Others prefer to keep it by a window, visible to charging sun rays. Finally, add items on your altar that reflect your purpose. Most altars will include the four elements—earth, air, water, and fire—which you can do through soil, incense, a bowl of water, and candles, respectively. From there, you can feel free to include mementos that are holy to you, including a Bible or other spiritual text, pictures of loved ones, special herbs, a journal, or crystals, to name a few. For some, your altar will become a space to sit, kneel, or stand in prayer and gratitude to God. For others, it will be where you meditate, practice rituals, or journal to connect and communicate with yourself or your ancestors. It may even be both and so much more. Regardless, altars are sacred spaces that nourish the spirit.

Maintain Your Relationships with Loved Ones Who Have Passed Away

Holidays like Día de Muertos and yearlong ofrendas are evidence that Latinas have long believed in maintaining relationships with loved ones who have departed from the physical realm, but these aren't the only ways to stay connected to someone who has passed away. Far from it.

The dead always accompany living loved ones, but you may not feel their presence immediately. How could you? Grief is all-consuming. It's like a tsunami, swallowing you whole and hurling memories around like debris. There are parts of yourself, those aspects you shared with the person you loved and lost, that you feel like you can't express or enjoy anymore, because doing so is now too painful. But, amor, this is how you stay close.

You carry on bonds with deceased relatives, friends, and partners by continuing to make them a part of your life. Many people do this by talking to their deceased loved ones aloud, writing them letters, keeping photos of them around their home, and celebrating their birthday and favorite holidays as if they were physically present. But you can also maintain these ties by preserving the activities you both enjoyed, like traveling, going to concerts, or watching silly rom-coms. Finishing projects that they were working on, whether they were fixing something in their house, creating scrapbooks for their child, or volunteering locally, is another powerful way to keep your lost loved one in your life. If it helps, consider dedicating one day out of your week or month to just be with them, frequenting the restaurant you two always dined at, rewatching a favorite show, spending time with their family, or crying into your journal. Your relationship is sacred; honor it and maintain it in a way that feels natural to you two.

If your grief is fresh, know that it may take some time to start feeling your loved one's presence again. But as you shift into new daily patterns, you will see that your relationship with them has not dissolved but rather has evolved. It's not the same, and definitely not how you prefer it. But it still grows spiritually, and you can nurture it with time and attention, just as you did when they were alive.

Find a New Hobby

As a Latina, you have probably been taught to prioritize your career and your family, leaving little room on your agenda to fit in a hobby. And, honestly, at a time when a "livable" wage can't really afford you much living, doing something fun for yourself might feel like a luxury. But, baby girl, that's a splendor that you deserve—and one that will nourish your soul.

A hobby is any activity you do for pleasure during your leisure time. It can be athletic, like learning tennis or joining an amateur softball league; creative, like taking a ceramics class or picking up your old guitar; or intellectual, like studying a different language or researching your family's history. These activities help you unwind from the pressures and worries of your everyday life and reinvigorate your spirit. Research shows that spending time doing activities that you actually enjoy improves your overall well-being. It reduces stress, promotes mental health, and strengthens relationships.

The two main reasons people don't treat themselves to a hobby are not having the money and not having the time. But enjoying an activity, like sports or literature, doesn't have to cost you anything. Consider shooting hoops at a local park or borrowing books from the library. If you need to spend some money, open a dedicated savings account just for this pastime. Next, see when you can fit this joy into your calendar. If you like to hike, explore a new trail monthly. If you enjoy making art, dedicate time weekly to your craft. And if you're keen on gardening and work from home, spend your workday breaks tending to your plantitas. Any effort you put into making this hobby happen will be well worth it when you see how happy and peaceful it makes you.

Observe Seasonal Changes

Generations ago, before modern calendars and clocks, your ancestors altered aspects of their daily life depending on the season. Farming, hunting, and foraging relied on the time of year. Spiritually in tune with Mama Tierra, they shifted work routines and social activities alongside the environment's natural changes, like flowers blooming in the spring and animals migrating in autumn. While industrial and technological advances allow you to now experience each new season with minimal interruptions to your life, intentionally observing seasonal changes can be spiritually rejuvenating.

Recognizing and honoring seasonal transformations reminds you that you are a part of a natural world where everything is cyclical. Some seasons bring cold deaths; others engender sunny rebirth. Even more, you are spiritually and materially connected to all living things—humans, animals. and plants. Being more conscious of this fact may inspire you to live more intentionally and sustainably.

Observing seasonal changes can look a myriad of ways. You may want to celebrate the shifts in seasons by planting cold-season or warm-season seedlings in your garden or incorporating produce that is in its harvest peak in your meals. If you prefer ceremonies, you may want to discover how Latin American spiritualities honor the energies of each season with herbal tonics, moon rituals, altar decorating, and other activities. Or perhaps you want to create new traditions altogether. However you choose to mark the new season, it will fortify your spiritual relationship with nature and yourself.

Pray

Prayer is an invocation to a higher power. For some, like Christians, Muslims, and Jews, it's a holy conversation between you and God. For others, it can be an appeal or expression of gratitude to an ancestor or a guide. Regardless of your religious or spiritual background, prayer is a powerful practice that can help nourish your mind, body, and spirit.

Studies have found that invoking a higher power that is both loving and protective can reduce feelings of anxiety and fear. Whether the relief is provided by metaphysical intervention or by casting your worries on another being, prayer can lift mental loads. Even more, this relationship with a divinity that loves, cares, and protects you makes you feel supported and less lonely. In this way, oración, like some other spiritual rituals, can be calming and renewing.

But if you didn't grow up praying, you might not know where to start. In truth, prayer can be practiced in so many beautiful ways. If you grew up en una iglesia pentecostal, prayer may be a full-body experience, conversing with the Holy Spirit through movement and tongues. If you were raised Muslim, perhaps you kneel down to pray five times a day. And if you follow Santería, prayer may incorporate candles, beads, or offerings. Prayer can accompany spiritual practices, like smudging with palo santo or during bathtub limpiezas.

Like these lovely traditions, and so many others, prayer can be ritualistic, but it can also be extemporaneous. It can usher you to a house of worship or a home altar, or it can be performed just as effectively on a walk, during a car ride, or while you shower. You can pray at certain times of the day, like in the morning, before meals, or during the evenings, or whenever you feel called. Prayer can express gratitude, petitions, or confessions. It can be a recitation, a song, a dance, or your own unscripted poem. Let your soul lead the dialogue.

Hold a Funeral for Your Past Self

Rituals are powerful. Whether they are repeated practices or performed a single time, rituals are material actions that mark transitions and help you release burdens. Take, for instance, funerals. These ceremonies that honor and mourn the life of someone who passed away denote the beginning of a complicated transition for all impacted by the loss. A funeral signals a new chapter, one perhaps of grief, solitude, and rebirth.

Recognizing how funerals symbolically move people along to a different phase in their life, more Latinas are starting to hold similar ceremonies for past versions of themselves. Whether you have just signed divorce papers or started working with a therapist to heal childhood trauma, these ceremonies allow you to grieve the loss or pain of a previous life. It doesn't mark the end of your suffering. Healing is not linear. But it can help spiritually prepare you for the journey.

First, set your intentions. What parts of your past are you saying goodbye to and how will this closure help you become the person you want to be? Next, decide if you want to do this alone or invite girlfriends to hold and celebrate you. Then, come up with an agenda. Oftentimes, self-funerals include burning rituals. You may want to smolder photos of your past self, set fire to an old wedding dress, or write a letter and set it aflame to release complicated feelings. Just make sure to include an activity that symbolizes your dedication to resurrection. By letting go of the person you once were, you create space for the bright, beautiful being you're ready to become.

Nurture Your Green Thumb

Have you ever watched abuelita tend to her plants? Whether she was singing to her house plantitas as she watered them or frolicking around outdoors in her pava while she tidied her garden, abuela radiated brighter than the sun—and not just because the rays glistened on her skin. That glow emanated from the inside, revealing a euphoric soul.

Working with plants and herbs nurtures your mind, body, and spirit. Outdoor gardening combines physical activity and social interaction with nature, strengthening your muscles, bones, and immune system while also making you feel more at ease and joyful. For Latinas, planting the veggies you consume can also foster a sense of agency and justice as you mend your own health outcomes and push back against inequities in the corporate food system. But you don't have to grow a jardín to experience the health benefits of greenery. House plants are also therapeutic, reducing stress and anxiety and boosting your immune system and mood.

To develop a green thumb, first figure out what kind of greenery fits your current lifestyle. Do you travel a lot for work? Perhaps low-maintenance plantas are best for you. Do you want to start growing your own food but don't have a yard? Start by sprouting herbs like cilantro and culantro from inside your home or joining a community garden. Have more space to spread out? Plant flowers, shrubs, or trees and turn your yard into a private oasis.

Next, educate yourself on how to germinate and grow plantitas. Certain plants do better in certain climates. Drought-tolerant plants like succulents and cacti thrive with minimal maintenance in dryer climates like that of Texas, while tropical plantitas like hibiscus flowers and ginger lilies flourish despite the high temperatures and humidity in states like Florida. If you live in an environment that's similar to your country of origin, consider growing plants that are native to your homeland. Lean on the knowledge of your abuelita, mami, tía, or comadre. Learn by watching them work with nature. If you're the first to reclaim this ancestral tradition of plant work, there are numerous guides and educational videos online.

Finally, spend time with your greenery. Feel your plant's soil and identify any changes in its leaves. This is how it communicates what it, and maybe even what you, need. It's how you nurture each other.

Revitalize Your Spirit
with Childlike Play

What did you enjoy playing as a child? Were you into enchanting fairies? Did you pretend to be a Disney Princess? Maybe you put together colorful costumes and makeshift stages to perform a song, play, or choreography for your family (or your stuffed animals). Or perhaps you liked to get dirty, dissecting bugs in the backyard or sliding to third base on your Little League team. You had something (or several things) that sparked your creativity and made you feel alive. And then, as you got older, you became too grown, too cool, too smart, or too busy for these activities. Interestingly, it's around this time that life may have also started to feel too humdrum. That's not a coincidence.

Looking at your never-ending to-do list, play can feel like a waste of time. You've exhausted yourself with productive activities, so why would you do something silly that doesn't help you meet one of your many goals? The answer: because you deserve to do something that's just for fun.

Enjoying a carefree activity that's imaginative and entertaining regardless of its end result is just as important to your well-being as an adult as it was when you were a chamaquita. Playfulness helps you unwind. A study published in the journal *Leisure Sciences* found that playing can help you cope with stress and anxiety. Playful behaviors also encourage creativity, gratitude, hope, excitement, and laughter.

To enjoy the benefits of playtime, reflect on the activities that filled you with unabashed excitement as a kid and recreate them today. Maybe you like to bedazzle clothes or sing karaoke. Or perhaps you prefer to play Uno, build sandcastles, or climb trees.

Hold yourself accountable by blocking out moments in your calendar for play. You can have fun by yourself, like playing a post-work dance video game, or turn play into a group activity, like hosting monthly game nights with trivia, cards, or board games. Also, take advantage of playful opportunities. The next time you watch your niblings, offer to play hide-and-seek. Give your inner child the permission to have fun without regulation.

Support Latine-Owned Businesses

When you support Latine-owned businesses, you deepen your spiritual connection with your community. By buying Latine, you improve your folks' financial well-being by helping them earn more money, create jobs, increase wages, build generational wealth, and close the racial and ethnic wage gap. When you give your coins to local companies and shops whose owners look or sound like you, people who may have faced more challenges to build and maintain their small businesses, you empower them. You contribute to the success of someone else from the block. Your community benefits, and as a member, you do too.

To support Latine-owned businesses, start with the items and services you usually spend money on. If you work from a café every weekday, frequent one that's Latine-owned. If you do compras every week, start food shopping at your local Latine-owned supermarket instead of the bigger retailer. If you get monthly facials, work with a Latina esthetician. And if your house needs a tune-up, hire a Latine contractor. Search online for specific Latine businesses or professionals servicing your area. If you don't find any, consider making online purchases.

Latinas, specifically, are behind a surge of new businesses. From apparel and cosmetics to home decor and wellness, there are so many stunning and sustainable products to choose from. And every time you wear or use these items, your spirit will radiate knowing you invested in the financial wellness of your community.

Call Your Loved Ones Who Live Abroad

Do you have a loved one who lives overseas or beyond an imaginary border? In the United States, one-third of Latines migrated from a different country, leaving behind family and friends. And even those who were born in the contiguous US have relatives in countries and territories throughout Latin America and the Caribbean, some they never met in person, others they see on occasion, and some who they may have been abruptly separated from due to a broken and unjust immigration system. Maintaining these long-distance relationships isn't easy, but it can be absolutely essential to your well-being.

According to the American Psychiatric Association, family separation, especially related to detention, deportation, and forced migration, can cause long-term trauma and increases the risk of depression, anxiety, and PTSD. While healing from this severance may require support from a mental health professional, ensuring that you and your loved ones are still actively a part of each other's lives despite the distance can help ease some of the hurt and loneliness.

To start, schedule regular calls a few times a week or a month. Having these phone or video chats on your calendars ensures both you and your loved one will be available, and hopefully not distracted, during the conversation. You can also start or add them to a family or friends WhatsApp group chat to share updates and photos throughout the day. On that, stay up on their country's current affairs so that you're abreast on issues they may be concerned about. Hearing your loved one's voice or seeing their face light up through a video call could be spiritually restorative for the both of you.

(Re)learn Your Mother Tongue

Do you struggle to speak your heritage language? It's a common experience for Latinas. Language is one of the first aspects of somebody's culture that is lost while acculturating. And the reasons are multiple. If you speak one language, like English, more than your heritage tongue, then you are more likely to forget the latter's vocabulary and grammar. Even more, speaking nondominant tongues, like Spanish, Portuguese, Haitian Creole, and Indigenous languages, in public can be dangerous. Xenophobic attacks against people who speak these languages are up, and while being multilingual generally improves someone's cognitive abilities, it's not always seen this way on school campuses and in workplaces.

Regardless of why you're not fluent in your mother tongue, it can still cause shame. To be clear, language does not make you more or less Latina, especially one that was forced on your ancestors through colonization, but the guilt of not being able to communicate with an elder or the embarrassment of not being able to check bilingual on a job application still stings. Learning, or relearning, your heritage language can strengthen your relationships with people you love, enable you to enjoy new entertainment, and help you read about your history from its original authors—all nourishment for your soul.

To start, first cut yourself some slack. Remember that this language (which may have been imposed on your predecessors) was taken from you. Also, recognize that you probably know a lot more than you think you do. Next, decide why you want to know this language. Do you hope to do work for communities that will require you to speak it? If so, you might want to enroll in a language-learning class or hire a teacher. If you want to be able to communicate with loved ones, try language-learning apps, consume media in that language, and speak it as much as you can throughout your day so you feel more comfortable. Finally, focus on the joy. Don't make this another thing to beat yourself up about, mama. Have fun with it. Learn songs in your heritage tongue. Frequent bars, churches, or bodegas where that language will be spoken. Celebrate yourself for how far you've come.

Excavate Your Family History

Being Latina can feel isolating sometimes. You're not reflected in mainstream media often, especially if you're Black and/or Indigenous, and you might be the only one in your workplace or classroom. But even if you're surrounded by your culture and people who look or sound like you, there's always this sense of not belonging, this feeling of being neither from here nor there, ni de aquí, ni de allá. Excavating your family history can help you find your place, your home within yourself.

Your presence is a gift that so many people had a hand in making. Just as you navigate your life across intersections, your ancestors also belonged to different communities. They came from different nations, spiritualities, and professions. They were likely of different races, spoke distinct languages, and had different abilities. Learning your family history teaches you about who your ancestors were during other periods and in other places, helping you understand what their lives were like.

For Latinas especially, discovering your ancestral lineage is a forced reckoning. In your family history, you might find colonizers and colonized people, enslavers and ancestors who were enslaved, and oppressors and those who've been oppressed. Uncovering these contradictory histories is complex and emotional, but it's still a gift. Knowing whose stories you carry with you allows you to consider which ones you want to carry forward, guiding you as you live your own life, and whose wrongs you want to amend.

To start exhuming your ancestral history, talk to your family. Ask them about elders that you never met, have them share their migrational journeys, and learn the familial surnames that didn't make their way to you. Complement these oral histories with research. Discover what life was like for people like your ancestors in the location and age they lived. To dive deeper into your genealogy, you may have to spend some money. For instance, there are digital databases and in-person archives that you might have to pay subscriptions to access or travel to visit. But there are also free resources, like FamilySearch.org, and public libraries that give you access to the pricier Ancestry.com without cost.

As you undergo this project, so many feelings may come up for you—sorrow and shame as well as joy and pride—but through it all you will feel spiritually activated, like your soul is in conversation with the spirits of those who came before you.

Discover the Heroines of Your Homeland

Did you read about your cultural history in school? If you grew up outside of your family's homeland and didn't enroll in Latin American or Caribbean courses in college, then you probably did not. Depending on where you went to school, your teachers might've tossed around names like César Chávez or Che Guevara, but it's unlikely any of them took the time to teach a nuanced lesson about either of these men—and it's even less likely that they mentioned the legacies of historic Latinas. And not learning about these people, places, and events might have misled you into believing that this history was not worth telling and, thus, not worth knowing, that there were no legends and heroes. But, mama, that's so untrue.

Across Latin America and the Caribbean, there are stories of people-powered revolutions that transformed society, women who defied patriarchal governments to expand gender equality, and inventions that improved the way of life for people all over the world. Latina heroes of the past range from Nicaraguan telegraphist and revolutionary Blanca Aráuz, who resisted US imperialism; to Haitian lieutenant Sanité Bélair, who organized enslaved populations to join her in the army of Toussaint Louverture to defeat French colonial rule during the Haitian Revolution; to Felícita Campos, a Black Colombian farmer who sparked a land rights movement after the government tried to steal her property.

To start studying the history of your land and its people, read books and peer-reviewed articles. Scour libraries, bookstores, and online databases like Google Scholar for biographies, books, articles, atlases, and newspaper archives. There may even be documentaries, films, or podcasts dedicated to this history. Start by streaming series like *Celia*, the telenovela about the life of Afro-Cuban salsera Celia Cruz, and documentaries like *Dolores*, about Chicana labor rights leader Dolores Huerta, as well as listening to podcasts like *La Brega*, which uses narrative journalism to share Puerto Rican history and experiences, and *AfroDiastories: Black Latin American Histories and Futures*, where Black Panamanian host Dash Harris contextualizes current affairs with commentary on Black Latin American history. Finally, if you're able to, visit museums and historical sites throughout your origin country or territory.

Chances are you aren't the only one who didn't receive a comprehensive education on Latin American and Latine history in school. Connect with friends who share your intellectual interests and take historical deep dives together. Make history club the new book club by watching monthly documentaries, discussing books, or creating spaces to share knowledge with each other. Learning your history while in community will stimulate spiritual growth and fulfillment.

Learning the names and stories of heroines from your homeland will remind you that you come from a land where women who looked or sounded like you rebelled against colonialism, challenged social norms that sustained inequality, and cared for their communities. These inspiring narratives may both fill you with pride and call back your spiritual purpose.

Support Causes
You Care About

When you contribute to causes you care about, you support communities and yourself. Giving back elevates your mental, physical, and spiritual wellness, and not just because of those fluttering warm, tender feelings. Studies show that acts of altruism lower your blood pressure and stress levels and improve self-esteem, life span, and overall happiness. And more than that, meter mano connects you with other people and widens your worldview, raising your spirit higher than Mariah Carey's iconic "Emotions" note.

To start, make a list of the issues that you are passionate about and decide which ones you will actively participate in. With so many communities under attack, there may be several matters that you care about, but you might not be able to be involved in all of them. For instance, you might care deeply about aiding migrants at the border, housing queer and trans youth, or funding abortions for people who need and can't afford them, but because of your lived experiences, you might choose to focus your energy on supporting disabled elderly people or teens whose parents are incarcerated. This is totally okay. You can volunteer at an organization that serves seniors or mentor a high school student whose mom is behind bars while still staying abreast and uplifting the work others are doing around different social issues that matter to you.

Once you've chosen the cause or causes you want to focus on, think about how you will invest in them. Will you volunteer at a local organization? Will you donate regularly to mutual aid groups back in your homeland? Will you create and disseminate educational content about your cause or causes on social media? Will you mentor someone? Will you start a support group? Once you figure out the best way you can use your talents, insight, connections, and resources, research groups and efforts that are already active so that you don't have to start from scratch. Finally, to sustainably give back, find ways to fit service into your calendar and/or budget. This is about community wellness, and that means caring for yourself, too, so that you don't have to burn out or go broke doing more than you can. Start by doing one effort a month. If you find that you can handle more, move to weekly or get involved with another issue that matters to you.

Whatever service looks like to you, it can bring deeper meaning and purpose to your life. So pour into your community and your spirit by giving back however you can.

Find Community

Ma, are you struggling to make friends? You're not alone. In a 2019 Evite study of two thousand people in the US, 42 percent reported that they had trouble making friends. In fact, the average adult hasn't made a new homie in five years. And it's not because folks don't want more companions. Actually, a lot of women are starving for friendship. But demanding work and life schedules, as well as recent work-from-home trends, have made it even more difficult to meet new people and invest time and care into relationships for them to grow. This is a problem because community is essential to your spiritual wellness.

Without amiguis, you are more likely to feel socially isolated, which can make you anxious and depressed and may even increase your risk of dementia and premature death. Conversely, research has found that developing and maintaining healthy friendships reduces loneliness, and the stress and anxiety that come with it; alleviates pain; and improves your life satisfaction. You deserve the kind of squad that heals and enlivens your spirit.

Unfortunately, finding community can be even more burdensome for you as a Latina. Be real; not anyone will do. You're not going to put up with microaggressions, and you shouldn't, and it's just not fun to be the only one at brunch without a ski trip story to tell. You know that community is sacred, and you're searching for kindred spirits who you can be your whole self with. Where they at?

First, know that no single person can, or should be expected to, be everything to you. You're a multifaceted mami. You have a range of experiences, talents, and interests. Who can match that? Instead, you can have different friendships that stimulate the different parts of you that make you whole. To forge new friendships, don't be afraid to do things solita. Enroll in an art seminar by yourself. Sign up for a volunteer group even if you're going alone. Show up to a Hot Girl Walk on your own. Pull up to those salsa lessons without a partner. When you stop waiting on someone else to do something that you want to do, you set yourself up to meet new people who enjoy those activities as much as you do. As you keep going back, you'll find yourself making new acquaintances. Exchange contact information and hang out outside of the setting that brought you two together. You might vibe or you might not. But if you do this often enough, you'll notice that your friend group is a lot fuller—and so is your spirit.

Nurture Your Relationship with Your Higher Power

What's your higher power? For some, it's Jesucristo, Yemayá, or Allah. For others, it's the universe, nature, or love. According to Alcoholics Anonymous, a higher power is anything that is greater than yourself, and connecting with yours can stimulate your spiritual wellness.

Research has found that maintaining a healthful spiritual relationship with a higher power can help you cope with everyday stress, feel connected and grateful, and live a longer life. Connecting to your higher power can be done in so many beautiful ways. There are traditions that are common across organized religions, like prayer, meditation, and congregation, and there are secular practices, like spending time in nature or serving your community. Regardless of the higher power you subscribe to, these activities can fill you with love, peace, clarity, and comfort.

Having a spiritual relationship with a higher power doesn't require you to practice a specific faith. You may have grown up in a fundamentalist home, experienced religious trauma, and lost your faith; but when you need a spiritual refill, you still turn to worship music like Jaci Velasquez's *Llegar a ti* album. Or you may be skeptical of religion and still find yourself drawn to learning and reclaiming the spiritual practices that were robbed from your ancestors. You could even be interfaith, recognizing the sameness in religions and spiritualities that have divided communities for too long.

You choose your higher power. Just nurture this spiritual relationship so that your soul remains grounded no matter what your mind and body endures.

Date Yourself

Whether you're single, seeing multiple people, or in a committed relationship, you need to be dating yourself. Think about how exciting dates can be: You dress up and do your makeup to go out for a fun activity and conversations with a cutie. When you get back home, you either flutter about or ponder if you actually like this person. Dating yourself can be just as rousing and introspective—and even more spiritually worthwhile.

When you hang out with someone you matched with on an app, you'll spend hours learning about each other. Similarly, when you're dating yourself, you can spend that time getting a better sense of who you are: your likes and dislikes, your goals and regrets, and your love languages and nonnegotiables. You are figuring out what matters most to you. And because you're listening to yourself, you're also able to enjoy some self-romancing. Just as someone who is trying to impress you might pay for your meal or buy you roses, you can treat yourself. You can take yourself out to dinner and a movie. You can write yourself love letters. You can make yourself a playlist. You can buy yourself heart-shaped chocolates and bath salts. And you can slip into your sexy lingerie and bask in solo intimacy.

Self-dating is like un jugo de parcha. It's refreshing, sweeter as it ripens, and jam-packed with nutrients. But it's you who have the juice, and when you pour that juguito back into yourself, you nourish your spirit. When you take time to date yourself, you are putting energy into caring for and appreciating yourself. You are less concerned with people-pleasing or being liked by others because you already have the person whose opinion matters most: you. You build self-awareness, confidence, independence, and happiness. So dedicate a classic by Eydie Gormé y Los Panchos to yourself and have some flowers sent to your home. Be the own love of your life.

Hang with Your Homegirls

Janguear con tus girlies is more than just fun—it's medicine. If you have your own group of homegirls, then you've undoubtedly experienced this social remedy already. When you're with your girlfriends, women who you can be your full self around, your mind is unburdened, your body feels safe, and your spirit is loved. It's a wholly revitalizing experience.

Healthy female friendships, the kind of all-girl corillo that gives and takes in equal measure, can help you live a fuller and longer life. According to a study out of UCLA, when you as a woman experience stress, you release oxytocin, a hormone that compels you to "tend and befriend." In other words, when you're stressed, your body craves social connection; it wants to be held down by your community. And homegirls do just that. They provide a space for you to destress without judgment and nurture you back to emotional equilibrium. A study published in the *Journal of Epidemiology & Community Health* found that older people who have a clique of friends have a longer life span than those who don't have much companionship. Even more amazing? A study in the journal *Cancer* determined that non-white women with breast cancer who have strong relationships are more likely to survive; actually, friendship has a greater effect on health than a relationship with a spouse or relative. Your girl gang is really *that* powerful.

Unfortunately, more women, including those who have several girlfriends, say they feel lonely, and it's because they're not spending time with the girlfriends they do have. Researchers at Oxford University recommend that you hang out with gal pals at least two times a week to maintain social nourishment. But with demanding life and work schedules, getting the girlies together this often is difficult.

Nonetheless, making time to connect with your homegirls must be a priority. If you need to, schedule weekly or monthly meetups or virtual calls. You don't have to all be together all the time. Take a bachata class and try out a new Latin American or Caribbean restaurant with one girlfriend, and go on your walks, hikes, or gym sessions with another friend whose schedule matches yours. To get all the mamis together, host monthly game nights, seasonal potlucks, or annual girls' trips. When you're together, notice your mind ease, your muscles loosen, and your spiritual vibrations rise. Again, sisterhood is medicine.

Embrace Your Accent

A lot of Latinas carry accents when speaking. If you have one, what does yours reveal about you? Maybe the Spanish, Portuguese, Haitian Creole, or Indigenous language tangled in your tongue announces your emigration from a land in Latin America or the Caribbean. Or perhaps the Nueva Yol, Flawda, Tejas, or *like* San Fernando Valley inflection unveils your upbringing in a historically Latine neighborhood in the US. How lovely it is to represent your barrio, the home that made you who you are, with every utterance.

If only the rest of society saw it that way. In a colonized land governed by the descendants of British settlers who imposed their language and culture on Indigenous communities, English remains a symbol of intellect and decorum. Even though the US does not have an official language, language and accent biases are everywhere. Speaking English with an accent that tells your migrational story could impact the way people think about you. A study at Brigham Young University found that people who speak with accented English, particularly with hints of dialects outside of Europe, are perceived as less intelligent and less trustworthy. And worse, these groundless, xenophobic, and racist assumptions limit the access people with accents have to housing and jobs.

And how has society responded to this? Instead of challenging accent bias, there are accent reduction courses available that charge you to remove your homeland from your tongue. Colonial capitalism. Mami, don't appease them. Your money and time can be better spent. Unlearn the shame tied to your accent. Embrace the way your intonation and enunciation color the English language.

Celebrate your ability to transition between languages or represent your 'hood by simply opening your mouth. You can do this by:

- *Speaking up during those moments when you may have previously let your insecurity around your accent keep you quiet.*
- *Recording yourself reading your favorite poem and listening to the beauty of your voice when you play it back.*
- *Defending yourself if someone treats you differently because of how you speak.*

To be spiritually well is to accept the fullness of who you are, and this includes your gorgeous accent.

Correct the Mispronunciation of Your Name

Your name is so much more than a designation. It's a gift from your family. It's a way for your ancestors to survive through you. It renders you visible, roaring "presente." So when someone mispronounces your name, especially after you've corrected them, it feels like a slight, like an attempt to minimize or erase you, your lineage, and your culture. And that ain't right.

For Latinas, and for other immigrants and communities of color, name mispronunciation creates shame that starts young. A study published in the journal *Race Ethnicity and Education* found that young people endure humiliation, anxiety, or shame when their names are pronounced incorrectly in class. Each mispronunciation signals that your name is too complicated and that you aren't worth the effort of rectification.

As an adult, that inner child is triggered every time someone says your name incorrectly, laughs that they just can't seem to get it right, attempts to anglicize it, or gives you a nickname to avoid calling you by your name altogether. But you're not going to be disrespected anymore. If someone says your name wrong, correct them. If it helps, come up with phonetic spellings of your name or share a familiar word that rhymes with your name. Release any shame you might have internalized about the name your family blessed you with and demand that people respect it. This is how you claim your dignity. This is how you honor your spirit.

Look at Yourself Through Decolonized Eyes

Have you ever looked at yourself through decolonized eyes? When you remove the Eurocentric, ableist, male gaze you've been taught to see yourself through, you can focus on the ancestral narratives behind your facial features, skin color, hair texture, and body type. You're stunning, mami—a rare, invaluable, and genuine work of the most masterful of artists.

As a Latina, you are confronted with at least two unattainable and conflicting beauty ideals. A Latin American standard that favors whiteness and slim frames with large breasts, round hips, and fat derrieres, and an Anglo one that praises Eurocentric features with lean bodies. Not fitting into one or both of these racist and unrealistic ideals can make you feel undesirable and, worse, unworthy. This is detrimental to your spirit.

If you're struggling to see the true version of yourself, free from colonialism's violent beauty myths, have a self-photoshoot. Be both the woman behind the camera and the subject in front of the lens. Create your scene and style yourself so that you feel comfortable—no, glorious—as you dazzle the camera. Take several shots. When you're finished, put the camera away and return to it after a day or so. Swipe through the photos. Know that you may not like them all, but there will be some that leave you in awe. Your distinct allure; you see it now. Gaze at these images for as long as you'd like, and return to them whenever you need to be reminded of the beauty you are—outside and in. You are so much more than how you look, but you can find power and beauty when you look at yourself with decolonized eyes.

Go to a Concert or Music Festival

Listening to music is a spiritual experience. It has the power to shift your mood and bring you back to yourself. When Celia Cruz's "La Negra tiene tumbao" blasts from the stereo, Black Latinas dance, aware of their resplendence. When Karol G and Shakira's "TQG" plays, the newly single mamis dry their eyes and shake their derrieres. Music helps you process and regulate emotions, and when it's experienced live, it can be transformative.

Live music is restorative. A study by researchers at Deakin University in Australia found that people who regularly attend musical performances have a higher sense of well-being than those who don't. Being outside of your house at a show where an artist you love is performing music that you have personal memories attached to releases feel-good hormones like serotonin, dopamine, and endorphins. Singing along with your favorite musicians reduces stress and makes you feel bonded. When you're in a crowd with strangers who share your musical tastes, you also feel connected to a larger community. Remember the last time you were at a concert and you and the nameless fan next to you shared quips before the show, offered to get each other drinks, and then yell-sang all the lyrics to the setlist together throughout the night? You didn't leave with her number and you didn't have to. Experiencing live music together cultivated a connection that you'll never forget. Clapping, swaying, and singing in unison with everyone around you made you feel close to each other. You were in a venue filled with kindred spirits, and your soul was stimulated.

To experience this mental relief and spiritual elation more often, start attending more concerts and music festivals. You don't have to spend a lot of money. You can have a vitalizing experience singing and dancing along with your favorite artists and their fans from affordable nosebleed seats or even supporting local bands that cover the songs you love. It's sharing the elixir of music with a community of people that's most spiritually uplifting.

Enjoy Latine
Entertainment and Art

After surviving another day of exotification as a Latina woman, you deserve to consume media and art that make you feel like a regular, degular girl from the block. Watching people who look or sound like you on TV reminds you that you are not some mystifying other. Reading literature about people who share your cultural background helps you feel seen. Listening to podcasts by other Latinas affirms you. And exploring Latine art in your neighborhood fills you with a sense of belonging. This is the healing and renewing potential of the arts.

Unfortunately, because Latines have historically been kept out of the entertainment industry, and since the few creators who have made it past the gatekeepers have portrayed the same kinds of white Latine narratives, there aren't many films and TV series that capture the diversity and nuances of Latine families and stories. But if there's one that you love, like the 2000s TV classic *Taina,* the Emmy award-winning series *Pose*, or the more recent hit show *Wednesday*, rewatch it as many times as you'd like. Watching something you've already seen several times eases anxiety and allows you to unwind because you already know what to expect.

If you want to enjoy new art and entertainment that more accurately reflect Latine experiences across race, sexuality, migration, and ability, turn to literature. More Latinas are landing book deals and telling a range of fresh tales, from coming-of-age novels by Elizabeth Acevedo and Gabby Rivera and haunting horrors by Silvia Moreno-Garcia and Isabel Cañas, to historical fiction by Marisel Vera and Dahlma Llanos-Figueroa and the classics by Isabel Allende and Julia Alvarez.

Whether you're streaming a program from your TV, devouring a new novel, listening to a podcast, or attending a local art show, engaging with media and art that you feel represented in can help you navigate your own identities and experiences as well as make you feel less alone. This connection is so good for your soul.

Learn How to Listen to Your Intuition

Have you ever gone to a trusted guide to help you make a really tough decision, and, anticipating their sage advice, felt dreadfully disappointed when all they tossed you was the generic "trust your gut" tip?

Yeah, same. I'm not saying this isn't good counsel, but without direction, it is, well, pretty useless—because how can you trust your gut or listen to your intuition when you don't know what either sounds like?

According to psychologists, intuition is the ability to understand something immediately, without the need for conscious deliberation or reasoning. Scientists describe it as the process in which information can register in the brain without conscious awareness; mystics view it as downloads from a higher being or one's inner magia.

Regardless of the explanation you prefer, your intuition acts as your soul's GPS, guiding you in the direction you're supposed to take and sounding an alarm when you're off course.

Sometimes, intuition speaks loudly: You feel a tightness in your chest or a sickness in your stomach when you are about to go down a path that isn't right for you. Other times, intuition whispers: A route doesn't seem rational, but you still feel confident and excited about following it, and opportunities leading you to this seemingly unrealistic trail keep popping up. This could be your intuition signaling you to toss logic aside and trust that this is the path for you.

Trusting a feeling over logic isn't easy, but there are techniques that can help you build intuitional confidence:

- *Acknowledge your intuition every time it has something to say.*
- *Ruminate on your gut feelings during a bath or by journaling.*
- *Practice following your intuition with the less consequential decisions to make sure you're not confusing intuition with fear.*

Your intuit on exists to guide you to a destination that reawakens your spirit. It's time to follow its lead.

Broaden Your Horizons with Travel

When was the last time you traveled somewhere? Not for work, either. A trip where you disconnected from your professional and home lives to explore a different place and culture. What did that feel like? For many people, traveling, both in and outside of your country, renews the mind, body, and spirit. This is because when you pack your bags and viajas, you leave the stress and worries of your daily life back at home and get to be present in your new environment. In a relaxed state, you're more likely to rest, have fun, and feel satisfied.

And there are so many kinds of trips that nourish you in different ways. Solo travel helps you reconnect with yourself. It presents you with an opportunity to do what you want, when you want, without having to accommodate anyone else. With no distractions, you are able to focus inward, checking in on yourself and discovering new things about you.

Meanwhile, a girls' trip gives you the opportunity to nurture your relationships with your best friends. Whether you're turning up and exploring nightlife with the only women who can keep you out past 10 p.m. or you're unwinding on a spa vacation, you're with girlfriends who hype you up, hold you down, and bring out the best in you.

Finally, more Latinas are choosing to travel with their parents. During these trips, you get to build deeper relationships with the people who birthed and/or raised you, discovering who they are beyond their roles as your mami or papi. It's also a way to give back to the elders whose sacrifices helped make your life a reality. Being able to give them the gift of travel, something that may have been inaccessible to them before, is a way to express your gratitude and build beautiful new memories that they, too, will be grateful for.

However you travel, and wherever you go (your neighboring city counts!), you'll feel a deeper connection with yourself, your travel mates, and remote communities you may not have thought too much about previously, allowing your spirit to feel more alive and refreshed.

Leave a Job You Hate

Have you ever worked somewhere you felt was killing your soul? You dreaded having to clock in, struggled to complete the workday, and asked yourself how much longer you could withstand the pain of working there every time you left? Heard.

Quitting ain't easy. You probably depend on your paychecks to support yourself, and possibly your family, so pulling a no call, no show isn't realistic. And leaving a career, one that cost you an expensive college degree and years in the game to secure, is devastating. But these are no reasons to spend most of your waking hours in misery. Your life is worth more than that. Your spirit needs to be set free. It's time to heed the sound advice of 2000s R&B singer Olivia and "Bizounce."

But you have to be strategic. If your emergency savings account is Cardi B thick and can hold you and your dependents down for a few months, then this is your permission to give your two weeks' notice (or not) and leave that job behind. But most people can't afford to just take off without other work lined up. If you are part of that group, then it's time to start crafting your departure plan. First, figure out if you're over your job because of an abusive workplace environment or because the actual work doesn't serve you anymore. This will help your job search by letting you know if there is something you absolutely don't want to be doing anymore. If you're worried about letting go of a career you spent so much of your life dreaming about and working toward, know two things:

1. *Your work does not define you. You are so much more than what you do under capitalism.*
2. *Your skills are transferable. You will be able to find other work without going back to school. Your degree was not for nothing.*

Next, make any necessary updates to your resume, LinkedIn profile, or website. While your current job may not have been kind or stimulating, you can use the experience to upgrade your portfolio. Just be sure to keep your plans to yourself or share them only with your trusted network. Your colleagues don't need to know your plans. Be proactive, but discreet.

Finally, as you start your job search, stay open to other forms of employment as well. Do you have entrepreneurial interests that you've been downplaying? Now could be the time to bet on yourself. Or maybe you have an in-demand skill, like writing, editing, or graphic design, that could secure you regular freelance opportunities. If you can, start these side hustles while you're still working your nine-to-five so that you transition into this new work full time when you're able to.

To be clear, quitting your job, pivoting in your career, and starting your own small business aren't easy. But difficult isn't impossible. You are more than qualified, mujerón.

Lighten Your Spirit
with Laughter

Is there a better feeling than laughing? It's one of the only experiences where every part of you is elated. No other sensation or emotion can sustain when you're cracking up, just delight.

This is because laughter reduces stress hormones, like cortisol, epinephrine, and dopamine, and enhances feel-good hormones, like endorphins. And this natural euphoria is good for your body and spirit. Giggling increases your count of antibody-producing cells, strengthening your immune system, while all the wiggling, jumping up and down, and good-crying that comes from chuckling allows your body to release emotions and tension. While you're rolling on the floor laughing, your soul is lifted and content. Life feels great, even if yours is kind of a mess. And you deserve that respite.

So watch that John Leguizamo classic, get tickets to Aida Rodriguez's next stand-up tour stop in your city, and follow those social media accounts curating Latine memes that remind you of the first people to make you laugh: your hilarious Latine family. On that, go visit that tía who always has jokes, and be the loud and unabashed Latine table cackling at the restaurant. Laughing is your spirit rejoicing. So howl and roar, loud and without shame, to spread some of that joy around.

Light a Scented Candle

There's something magical about scented candles. The sound, smell, and sight of wax light are transformative, altering your mood in seconds. Burning a candle may sweeten your disposition or aid your relaxation. It can turn you on or help you focus. Some fragrances may even transport you to another place or time, a memory or a fantasy that elicits a range of emotions. Magia.

It's no wonder there are so many spiritual traditions that incorporate candle practices. From Sunday worship leaders to brujas, Latinas of many faiths believe that the smoke of a blazing candlewick carries prayers up to a higher power. So they set intentions, through oración, meditation, or affirmations, as candlesticks flicker.

Whether you want to use candles as part of a spiritual practice or to unwind from your day, the aromatic crackling of a scented candle can nourish your soul. To treat yourself, purchase a vegan candle from Latina-owned shops like Vela Negra, Bonita Fierce, or Soy Latina Candles. These brands carry velas that fly you to a Caribbean playa or a Mexican desert. When your package arrives, set and light the candle away from anything that is flammable and enjoy the spiritually invigorating experience. You can elevate the affair by running a warm bath, reading a book, or listening to soulful classics by La Lupe or Susana Baca. By lighting a scented candle, you'll feel your spirit begin to blaze too.

Index

About the Author

Raquel Reichard is an award-winning journalist and editor whose work has appeared on *The New York Times*, *Refinery29*, *Cosmopolitan*, *Bustle*, *Well+Good*, *Teen Vogue*, and other major news and lifestyle outlets. Her writing and reporting covers Latine body politics, culture, and music, exploring themes of wellness, bodily autonomy, colonialism, and diasporic belonging. Based in Orlando, Florida, Raquel is passionate about creating media and spaces where Latinas and women of color feel represented, heard, affirmed, and held. In addition to writing, she founded Borilando, an arts, culture, and education nonprofit serving Puerto Ricans in Central Florida, and she leads a monthly brunch for Latinas in media. Born in Queens, New York, and raised in East Orlando with her Puerto Rican parents and older brother, she enjoys singing to Taylor Swift, dancing to Bad Bunny and Frankie Ruiz, watching rom-coms, and hanging out with her nephew and niece. Learn more at RaquelReichard.com.